THE
WISDOM YEARS

A GUIDE TO INTENTIONAL AGING

David —
a great read
for the one who
lives it & gets it!.
Barbara Skye

Barbara 'Skye' Boyd

ISBN 978-1-64471-808-7 (Paperback)
ISBN 978-1-64471-809-4 (Digital)

Covenant Books, Inc.
11661 Hwy 707
Murrells Inlet, SC 29576
www.covenantbooks.com

For Tom, a man of mind and heart.
For Heather, a woman of compassion.
For Jennifer, a woman of spirit.

CONTENTS

An Invitation

Him not busy being born is busy dying.
—Bob Dylan

Aging is complex! With little fanfare, I completed my career as a university administrator and professor, retired from the duties of ministry, applied for my retirement package, and left the "institutional world" for what I believed would become the adventure of a lifetime. I was *so* ready for freedom—or so I thought.

After a year of "play," I quickly became mired in boredom and began to explore a variety of activities and experiences to help define and claim my senior years as valuable years. But none of the choices I made inspired me or urged me to move into my own sense of "calling" into the Wisdom Years. Though I was unfettered, I was also ungrounded.

To use the word "calling" may seem a bit strange to you, the reader, but I have come to understand that to become a wise person as we age, to age with courage and compassion is a calling of sorts. Seniors do not accidently become wiser as we age. This is a juncture in our lives requiring us to be more fully awake and aware than at any other time if we intend to possess a quality life and avoid squandering our final days. Thus, a calling—an urgency, a responsibility of sorts— to quest for wisdom becomes mandatory for those of us with the desire to participate with grace and grit in the latter portion of life.

The one thing about which I am confident at this moment in my own life is: I am *not* interested in "playing on the fringes" of the institutional world in order to keep my foot in its waters, so to speak. Many of my colleagues are choosing this option because they are unable to leave their careers behind and risk the unfamiliar dance of empty time, of becoming a senior. They are attached (even perhaps addicted) to the institutional world. Observing this phenomenon has set in motion for me a dawning of the importance of *courage* and *intention* to the aging process.

Let's back up a few months, if you would go with me. Last year a friend gifted me with the book, *Falling Upward* by Richard Rohr. I devoured it within days, reading nonstop. I felt like this book had been written for *me*! Fr. Rohr seemed to be addressing my quest: How should I quietly slip out of the *institutional life* (Fr. Rohr's language) and boldly step into the *intentional life* (my language) of my Wisdom Years? As I eagerly turned the pages, I knew I was ready to hear his message.

Upon completion of Fr. Rohr's book, I immediately formulated for myself four pilgrimages to take place in the year ahead. I made a vow: I do not want my seventieth birthday to slip up behind me with a whack! My desire is to intentionally acknowledge this transition into the Wisdom Years. (I am a Baby Boomer, and we are not wise until our seventies anyway. Up until then, it's an obsessive work ethic, complicated marriages and a great deal of confusion and pathos!)

The urge to pilgrimage began for me when I taught this topic to Religious Studies "freshers" (first year students) for over a decade at the University of Oklahoma. These eager Millennials seemed intimidated and bewildered by the idea of walking a pilgrimage to enhance one's spiritual or emotional life. Each semester my introductory course syllabus included a section on pilgrimages, in particular the well-known Camino Santiago de Compostela. Teaching about pilgrimages cinched a hidden desire in my heart to make this particular compelling walk at some point in my own life.

For several semesters, I required my students to read Paulo Coelho's *The Pilgrimage* as one of their assignments. And in those semesters when it was possible, as part of our course of study, we viewed the film *The Way* with the quintessentially talented actor Martin Sheen. By the time I retired from the teaching portion of my professional life, I was fairly steeped in the art of pilgrimage. The itch to walk a pilgrimage lodged itself in my mind as I moved from Oklahoma to Santa Fe, New Mexico to begin my retirement years.

Now, as a result of how deeply Fr. Rohr's words affected me, this book is written as my response to his wisdom. When I read his proposal about the two halves of life, an intense interior reaction saturated my soul: "I must act on what I have learned from this spiritual teacher." This book you hold in your hands concerns how to *act* when something profoundly affects the psyche and calls us to change our lives. What follows is the discovery of courage to engage my senior years of life. Courage for what? The courage to live a "bold and beautiful" life (language from poet David Whyte), even as we move closer and closer to our own demise.

The pages that follow are part adventure, part interpretation of the walking experiences, part insight and the changes that now inhabit my being as a result of the experiences that occurred during my seventieth year. I invite you to join me, no matter your age. For many people, the move from institutional life begins in the fifties. Precise age is not as much the issue as is making this critical transition into the Wisdom Years with awareness and mindfulness. My goal for you? I hope—I pray that you will create your own ritual or life marker for shifting from *institutional years* to *intentional years*, however you wish to acknowledge this inevitable transition.

As I intend to use these terms throughout the pages of this text, please allow me to clarify. The term *institutional years* seems fairly obvious. I am referring to those years of our lives spent involved in our education or training, employment, careers and the development of our significant relationships, including the advent of children into our lives. When I refer to our *intentional years,* I mean specifically those years post-employment and the shifts in family life known most commonly as "empty nest." This time of life is best labeled "retirement" or "the senior years" when we intentionally and freely choose how to spend time that is completely ours to exploit or engage.

To make this transition requires one essential action: to accept our professional and familial institutional years for what they were and to release that period of life to the past so we are free to move forward into the future. To age with intention means we trust in our future as devoutly as we did in our younger days with all those years of exploration, work and creativity ahead of us. Though we acknowledge now that the time ahead is less than what has been lived, the intentional years have the potential to be the years of life with the most quality and depth. This is the time of life when we might explore the hidden passions and interests that have lain fallow throughout our institutional years. The choice for adventure and purpose is ours.

Baby Boomers are particularly vulnerable to being attached (even possibly addicted) to their work, careers, titles, accomplishments. Our generation has been taught that we are valuable because of what we *do*, not who we *are*. Thus, to relinquish our work, walk away from that desk, business, classroom or office requires an unbridled courage we may not have recognized before our retirement date. We are the generation that invented the word "workaholic." We shredded marriages and the lives of our children with our affinity for climbing that invisible ladder to something we called "success" so that we could purchase things: homes, cars, vacations, stuff, and more stuff!

And now we are paying the piper because so many Baby Boomer seniors have no idea how to retire gracefully, with a sense of purpose and meaning, with intention. Releasing our work creates, for some, a massive identity crisis in the psyche that becomes difficult to fill. What do we do with ourselves once we are thrust into the portion of life that calls for "being-ness" rather than "doing-ness"?

This book is written to give you, the reader, the nudge you may need to *become someone new* as you acknowledge the shift taking place in your life. You do not have to accept my choice as yours. In fact, most folks from age fifty on would not be interested in the way I celebrated turning seventy—camping, hiking, travelling abroad, and walking. There are any number of ways you might choose to make pertinent this rite of passage into retirement life and the Wisdom Years.

Challenge yourself in a way you never have. Recover that bucket list of things you wish you had done when you were younger and determine which adventures still attract you. Take a risk; confront your fears. Use your imagination in a fresh way to set yourself onto the path of your own adventure, no matter what this might be. Dream wildly and big! As a thoughtful friend said recently, "Find the craziness that will make you feel alive!" Discover the courage and resilience to act on your instincts! Become mindful! The point is, imagine your life and then become it!

Perhaps the best way to guide us into the chapters ahead is with Fr. Rohr's words:

> No one can keep you from the second half of your own life except yourself. Nothing can inhibit your second journey except your own lack of courage, patience, and imagination. Your second journey is all yours to walk or avoid. My conviction is that some falling apart of the first journey is necessary for this to happen, so do not waste a moment of time lamenting poor parenting, a lost job, failed relationship, physical handicap, gender identity, economic poverty, or even the tragedy of abuse. Pain is part of the deal! If you do not walk boldly into the second half of your own life, it is you who do not want it.

Strong words, these. But deeply important to undergird an understanding of the intention of this book. Let's begin and see what happens for you!

INTRODUCTION

When you travel, you experience, in a very
practical way, the act of rebirth.
—Paulo Coelho

I am a lazy awakener. Usually as I climb up out of the cloudy well I have dug for myself during my night of sleep, I roll around in my mind what lies ahead for the day. It takes a while for my brain to reignite. But on this particular chilly Monday morning in November of my sixty-ninth year, I realize that nothing I am able to conjure about my day ahead inspires me to put my toes on the cold floor. "I've had it with this!" I mutter to myself. "I am *not* going to bed tonight until I have a plan for next year."

Since the following year I will turn seventy, I covet a grand adventure on my calendar, one that will scratch this itch I have and entice me to dream myself into an as yet untold story. Reading Fr. Rohr's book in conjunction with this restless urgency that infiltrates my psyche to *do something* about moving into the second half of life, I am ready to plunge ahead! After downing my glass of fresh orange juice and hurriedly consuming a sumptuous breakfast of oatmeal and blueberries, I trot off to the very desk where I am currently writing these words. I type "self-guided walking tours" into the subject line of my computer and watch with astonishment as resource after resource fills the screen. Okay, now we are getting somewhere!

Sorting through multiple sites, I realize that I have options! I could easily create a series of topical interests for myself for the year and travel in a way that will coincide with each given theme, mimicking the author of *Eat, Pray, Love*. Or, perhaps I should locate new mentors for my Wisdom Years by attending workshops and retreats with some of the most enlightened spiritual teachers in the country. Or, perhaps I could organize exotic walks with interesting people to lovely places I have not before seen.

All of these ideas resonate with my vision for the year. What takes shape over the next few days of research is a combination of these schemes that evolves into my "Wisdom Year" pilgrimages. To refine the search and planning, I ask myself what most connects me to life (besides my precious family). Nature! I am most alive when I am out of doors. Divine Creation appeals to me most when I am a participant in it. I have long been a hiker, backpacker, camper, walker, in-love-with-the-outdoors kind of person, even as a child. (I would do *anything* to satisfy my mother, finish my chores, and escape outside to play.) I return to my first notion of walking and hiking to set about the process of organizing pilgrimages that will smash my retirement doldrums. Fr. Rohr's book challenges me to peep over the wall into the second half of life with a sense of adventure and less dread. So...

First, I acknowledge with a bit of ego that I want to test myself physically. How strong will I be at age seventy? Will I still be able to camp and hike as I have done for so many years? Do I have the ability to pitch a tent, sleep on the ground, climb a Colorado 14er, walk for miles up a mountain—all things I did when I was younger? What am I actually capable of doing at my age, and what activities do I need to surrender? Do I dare to become a septuagenarian while remaining physically as active as I wish? What am I attached to at this stage of life that I need to release?

My primary task is to find someone who will go with me into the mountains of Arizona who can serve as guide and companion. After contacting a friend from Colorado about my proposal, Cleve steps up as a veteran hiker and camper. He has the time, the gear, and the inclination to appreciate a good camping trip, so I sign him up to serve as my guide in the backcountry of Arizona.

The first pilgrimage is set! I choose two books to take with me as literary guides on my trip: *Desert Solitaire* by Edward Abbey and *Leaving Church* by Barbara Brown Taylor. (More about these selections during the pilgrimage chapters.)

This pilgrimage reveals my aging abilities for stamina, strength, and courage.

Intuition guides me toward my second pilgrimage. As a closet poet myself, I have long followed the work of David Whyte, Irish English poet, speaker, and spiritual teacher. I decide to check online for what he might be up to only to learn that he offers walking/hiking tours that include daily poetry sessions with him. I apply and am accepted to his tour in the English Lake District of northwest England. This event, without a doubt, changes my life in ways I could never have imagined. First, my poetic muse that has long slumbered while buried in the academic world, awakens with a ferocity yet unknown to me. During this retreat my own poetic sensibility comes alive again and my soul begins to stir. My personal vows are affirmed and challenged.

To top off our daily poetry session, each day includes strenuous hikes in the mountains of the stunning Lake District green, wet, often foggy, and sternly challenging to even the best of hikers. Between the hours of listening to David's poetry, the music from his merry band of groupies, and the daily hikes, I am renewed and re-enlivened as if I were in my thirties again. For this pilgrimage I select David's book, *River Flow,* carrying it with me and reading poetry from it every day as my inspiration and meditation. (His book still lingers on my desk as part of my daily meditation discipline.)

This pilgrimage inspires a need to break and make new vows in my life.

My third pilgrimage begins on a train from London to Moreton-on-Marsh in south central England known as the Cotswolds. Joann, a dear friend and former parishioner agrees to share this pilgrimage with me, trusting my retirement madness to organize this tour for us in a way that ensures she will come out alive and be pleased she has joined me! Day after day of lovely walks in the idyllic countryside, through quaint villages, traipsing through fields of sheep and along miles of grey stone walls held together somehow by magic and time keeps us enthralled with our journey. Musty churches greet us in each village. Lunches take place in dark, low-ceilinged, wooden-floored pubs, filled with the laughter and chatter of rural Brits all around us.

Accents are thick, and my ears have trouble distinguishing all their words, though I fully understood the joviality of the patrons.

Because most American citizens notoriously believe we are free, entitled, and independent (and I am one of them), this pilgrimage offers me sheer surprise: Freedom. What could this feeling possibly mean? In the flash of a sunlit moment, I grasp the insight for this pilgrimage: *a sense of anonymity*, no fetters of institutional life binding me. A sense of complete autonomy—healing—washes over me as I stand in a wheat field somewhere between Broadway and Chipping Campden. (Yes, these villages truly exist. Look them up for yourself!)

I discover quite unexpectedly in a British bookstore the two books I read on this pilgrimage: *The Unlikely Pilgrimage of Harold Fry* and *The Love Song of Miss Queenie Hennessy*, both by Rachel Joyce. (More about these choices in the chapter on this pilgrimage.) These are both novels about a pilgrimage, an unrequited love and two lives healed because one lonely man took a risk to save a life, his own. On the day I walk to Winchcombe from Guiting Power, I actually become seventy years old. I am exuberant on this day as I walk under a brilliant sun!

This pilgrimage offers me the first taste of authentic freedom.

Finally, I end my year of septuagenarian pilgrimages in lovely, pristine Vermont. This area of the country reminds me of the 1950s with its antique barns, sugar maple trees, winding roads and forests encrusted with trees so thick I cannot see through them. Quaint houses and eclectic, tiny "mom and pop" shops dot the countryside. For this journey, my spouse joins me, sharing the rocky trails, lush landscapes and hospitality of the lovely bed and breakfast hosts, complete with apples and warm, homemade cookies constantly at our fingertips.

As I begin this pilgrimage, I have read two books that inform and shape my insights and experiences on this journey. The first is a national best seller, *Being Mortal* by Atul Gawande, a most necessary read for anyone over fifty. For most persons who will read my book, the Gawande book comes as a logical follow-up. His book deals quite directly with our final years and with death. There is no way, as I stare the seventies in the face that I am able to avoid those topics.

The second book came to me completely accidently as I stood in a local bookstore pondering what I should read to prepare myself for my final pilgrimage. I had no previous knowledge of this author or of this book, but it almost leapt off the shelf at me: *The Course of Love* by Alain de Botton, a most unusual read about the peculiarities and painful edges of love relationships. This book would become a bittersweet guidebook by the time I completed my fourth pilgrimage.

This pilgrimage compels me to acknowledge that the realities of aging inside our relationships include attachments that no longer serve us and must be released.

In the following chapters, I will share the stories of these journeys but with this caveat. While I am involved in daily hiking or walking tours with my body, a hefty interior pilgrimage invades my soul, heart, and mind. I do *not* for even one minute of this entire set of pilgrimages perceive any of this to be vacation, travelogue or even particularly fun. The discipline of nurturing and maturing my soul, mind, and body is not *that k*ind of experience. While my body suffers on the outside with demanding and strenuous walking and hiking, my interior self reflects, contemplates, meditates, ponders, struggles with the task of locating my Self—this being who is in the midst of changing not only from one decade to another, but from one worldview to another. David Whyte calls this phenomenon "becoming a stranger to ourselves." From being employed to being in retirement, from an institutional to an intentional lifestyle, my life is in complete disarray and readjustment. When this year of journeying is over, I recognize that I am now officially a senior adult. No Baby Boomer avoidance tricks will function any longer!

The first chapter of this book begins on a somber note. *Be prepared for this!* Aging comes with too many complexities to ignore. I do not write this book to provide a "kum ba yah" tale about aging. Thus, I do spend time naming and discussing some of the more demanding issues that can instantly block or trap all of us who wish to become intentional about the aging project. These issues offer little levity! But they are real, and all seniors know their capacity to debilitate us. But do not be disheartened. The very point of this book is to say something like this: "Okay, we know the vicissitudes of aging are real and often frightening. But we also know that at this stage of life, if we do our interior work, we can face these moments with courage and compassion. We can live our senior years with intention and joy."

This book is meant to encourage you to become brave in facing your own limitations of aging while becoming intentional about creating for yourself a meaningful, purposeful, mindful adventure into your senior years. This is a book about recovery and discovery. What are the possibilities and positives of aging? Who are we to *be* at this stage of life? What might we *do* with the tension of living as Baby Boomer older adults who are not ready to slow down? We are the generation that has been obsessive, even addictive, about our work life. We lived our professional lives at a fast pace and dragged our families along with us. How do we now accept losing our connections to our work while living bravely and with gratitude into intentional aging, and a new worldview? This book, in other words, is not written for the eternal pessimist or cynic. This book is written for the *hopeful realist* and the *inveterate adventurer.* For those of us who seek an interior life as ferociously as we desire external possibilities while we age.

After sharing the stories of my four pilgrimages, and processing the lessons I learned, you will arrive at the final chapter of the book. Here I offer my own thoughts about the *Wisdom Years* of life that are ahead for those of us who dare to accept the challenge of aging rather than giving way to the darkness. My deepest yearning for this journey through my seventieth year is for this process to reveal an awakened transition into the second half of my life. I am not seeking an ending, but rather the beginning of a new personal story, one not yet carved into my psyche. In these pilgrimages I desire to risk my comfort zone for something unknown that will resurrect my deepest fears, my insecurities, my unknown self so that I might face these as I age. I covet a rebirth!

In these pages ahead I offer you the opportunity for a chance at transformation for yourself. These pilgrimages become, for me, the roadmap into my interior life at a whole new level, demanding that I decide what sort of "Elderly" I wish to become. This adventure is my quest to live bravely into the years ahead, for the senior years require courage most of all. I desire this for all of you who wish this for yourself.

A reminder from Fr. Rohr:

If you don't walk into the second half of your own life, it is you who do not want it.

Chapter 1:
Dilemmas of Aging
Stepping across the Line

Sometimes with the bones of the black sticks
left when the fire has gone out—
someone has written something new in the ashes of your life.
—David Whyte

Looking back has never been of much interest to me. It's too easy to step into a pothole when you are looking over your shoulder. I decided a long time ago that I would live as a "looking forward" kind of person. Somehow, to my way of thinking, life has more adventure ahead than what lies in the tracks behind me. When I reflect on this idea, I imagine standing in a curve in the middle of a winding road, in the autumn foliage of Vermont. Trees all around me are dressed in brightly colored leaves dancing in the wind, anticipating their chance to fall and become part of the vivid canvas on the ground. I see the road behind me where I have just walked, as I feel a touch of rare loveliness scattered about me. But for some reason, my particular psyche is more interested in what is around the next bend—that curve in the road where I am unable yet to view beyond the colorful, dangling leaves. What is ahead? What is it that beckons me forward into pure adventure and challenge? I am curious.

One bright blue-sky morning after my spouse and I have retired to Santa Fe, New Mexico, I awaken wondering "Is this all there is?" My retirement of three years has been pleasant enough (somewhat like permanent vacation), but something is also missing: a sense of purpose and meaning to this new phase of life. While I love being able to do what I want, when I want, with whom I want, wherever I want, I also feel a vague restlessness inhabiting my bones. I have been away from the institutional world just long enough to realize that twenty or more years of this retirement life could grow a bit tedious to someone like me who has always been busy, active, involved, engaged in life itself. As a person full of a sense of vision and adventure, curiosity and compassion, this newly found freedom is just *not* going to work for me if all it means is doing what I choose to do all day every day for the rest of my life.

Thus, I engage in the fatal mistake that so many Baby Boomers make who are living in the "second half of life" (Fr. Rohr's term): I return to a version of one of my former career paths (as pastor) with a caveat that this time the work will be short-lived and not as intense or stressful as past employment had been. The joy with which I had engaged my professional years does not emerge in this new situation. I am soon disenchanted. In a matter of months, I withdraw from that position and once again begin to flounder. I find at this juncture that I want to keep working (because as a Baby Boomer senior I don't quite know how to stop), yet I am completely dissatisfied with going backward into my former career track.

Next I try volunteer work for a year. Surely this will settle my inner rumblings about how to retire effectively and feel like I am still "part of the game." So many of my friends pursue volunteer work—and this is a *good* thing. Right? Retirees often have energy, time, vision, and enough financial stability to share their talents in such rewarding ways. In no way am I criticizing this model of retirement as I confess that for the moment volunteering does *not* do for me what it does for many of my friends. Oh, I do feel that my actions did matter for those people whom my years of service touched, but deep within I know this is *not* what my own heart and mind are seeking, at least at the current time.

Many spiritual teachers speak of the importance of service in this senior phase of life. I get this! But somehow, for me, volunteer work almost seems as if I am going backward in my life, as if service is a place holder in my bonus years to keep me feeling alive and of use to the human community. As I share this feeling with a friend of mine with some guilt and shame attached to it, her response resolves my confusion. Speaking rather forcefully, she says, "Skye, you have given your time and energy to other people all your life. You are just tired of that type of work at the moment." Like a lightning bolt her words struck me. As a counselor, pastor, and teacher, I have been involved *in service* in the institutional world for over thirty years of my life. Of course I am tired of this! Doing without pay what I have done for years for pay does not seem to be rewarding or fulfilling. No, somehow I am not yet on the path that my soul desires for stimulation, fulfillment, and purpose. I am in need of another trail to blaze during this early portion of my senior years.

On a local level, a dear friend of mine who is in her seventies spends hours and hours doing volunteer work each week with churches, homeless shelters, Habit for Humanity, providing meals for those who need to be fed and more. Another friend, who was formerly a teacher, assists an organization to aid immigrant children in learning English. Another has found her calling by taking a homeless family who lived in a car, housing them, placing the younger children back in school, and supporting one daughter in college. Several neighbors have discovered politics as their path of service and are embroiled for hours each day working on behalf of their sense of justice in the political arena. It is not at all uncommon for seniors to gravitate toward service as the way to find meaning in the years after retirement. What I fail to discover at this point in the story is the *type* of service that will be required of me as I age. More on this in the final chapter of the book.

So let this be my disclaimer: volunteering and service projects resonate deeply with many seniors, including myself. But this does not mean all retirees must follow suit. The point is this: What you may choose to do to create a sense of meaning and purpose in your Wisdom Years is quite personal to each individual and cannot be taken as a rule for everyone. Thus, at this point I am going to relinquish judgment about whether or not I should be involved as a change agent or even what kind of service might someday appeal to me. For now, at the beginning of this pilgrimage year, this will not be my quest.

Fr. Richard Rohr (mentioned in the Invitation) makes it abundantly clear in his book that in order for retirees to be in control of the "second half of life," we must admit that we are actually *in* this stage of life. We are advised to wake up to the gift of these senior years and recognize that they actually come to us with great benefit and responsibility. A portion of the task of self-discovery, according to Fr. Rohr, should actually begin within the closing years of institutional life, and continue on during the intentional life. With gratitude I realize that Fr. Rohr has challenged me to the discipline of locating my own sense of calling and purpose for these later years of life. And I have become quite aware that it is easy to miss this obvious point: The move into the Wisdom Years invites us to release our former life and then become deliberate and intentional about the next stage of life. The task immediately comes into focus: Awaken! Envision! Respond! So how to do this? How might we discover our second half of life "calling" without falling into the trap of repeating the first half of life? How and what do we bring to our later years that will allow these years to blossom into wisdom and fulfillment?

Over these past three years, I have conversed with several friends and acquaintances who have either kept their foot in the waters of professional life or have become heavily involved in volunteer work. Others have become permanent keepers of grandchildren, and still others have taken to golf courses or cruise ships. Watching these friends make their choices for retirement, I have felt as if so many have made these decisions in order to escape the reality that the later years truly do seem to move along, more swiftly actually, than we can even imagine. (This despite what Alan Burdick says in his book, *Why Time Flies* that I take up later.) For some, these decisions are life enhancing and meaningful, but for others, such activities are fillers as they struggle to find a role or a setting for their retirement life that provides a sense of satisfaction.

Before I move into the deeper purpose and perspective of this book, we must consider some of the key problems that arise during that walk across the bridge from "hanging out" in retirement to living into the depth of our Wisdom Years. What problems, you might ask? How can retirement possibly be a problem? But for many seniors, this time of life becomes quite troubling and complicated. To understand why I would take up walking as my way of building meaning for my early retirement years, I wish to lay out the key issues that I sense plague many retirees. These issues can disrupt our retirement years that should be about freedom and creativity and wisdom.

As I face some of these matters for myself, I realize how daunting the task of retirement will be if I do not grab hold of my life and become intentional about what fills my days and inspires my soul. It's a daily battle not to surrender to the demands of aging, and no one tells us this. I assume most of you, like me, have not been mentored in how to age with grace, vitality, and wisdom. For the most part we find ourselves simply flung into the fray of days with time on our hands and no one to answer to. We actually have to live out each day of our retirement years without having access to previous experience as an aging person. Not an easy task for any of us! Thus I wish to clearly state the tangible and problematic issues around aging in order not to "hide" what is true about this natural phenomenon we will all experience if we live long enough. Simultaneously, I invite you to resist the urge to surrender these most valuable and interesting years of life into the stormy seas of growing older.

The process by which we might seek to stay connected to our institutional lives in order to create a present life can easily become an obsession, which only makes us *tired, frustrated, angry, or sad.* Having tried this option for myself, I learned a few lessons from this failed experiment. Trying to recapture our previous professional successes usually creates fatigue, both mentally and physically, because fifty, sixty, seventy, and even eighty-year-old bodies do not work at the same pace as our younger bodies. (My fifty-plus-year-old stepson learned this hard lesson recently when he took on too much stress and ignored the signals sent to his worn-out body.) We need more sleep, less stress, meditation and yoga (or their equivalents in a religious life), better diet, and more life-enhancing alternatives in these years than we did in our younger years. *Fatigue* is a killer in the later years of life. It becomes quite easy to spot the flagging energy in our fellow retirees who have signed up for one too many projects, the seductive ploy designed to avoid empty time. Adequate rest and healthy life habits become even more critical as we age.

If we stay attached to our institutional lives beyond the burn-out phase, *frustration* begins to insert itself into our work. Seniors generally covet a broader set of interests to explore as they age. We are not so focused on forging a successful career, acquiring the pro-verbial mortgage and two-car lifestyle, raising kids and helping them through college until they are also happily launched. For most even financial acquisition loses its attraction. The retirement years may now include new friendships, recreational time, volunteer activities, the desire to complete our "bucket lists," an urge to take up never-be-fore-tried and only fantasized talents (like my friend who has taking up throwing pottery with a vengeance). To fill up this bountiful free time with too many obligatory activities steals well-deserved time and attention away from those aspirations we have put off for years and years. The Wisdom Years often give birth to an urge to be cre-ative, usually in a way not previously experienced. Frustration arises when we thwart this longing by clinging too closely to our former institutional patterns and ties.

Anger can pierce our retirement bliss because time does seem to accelerate toward our demise as we age. The "Elderlies" (as my granddaughter calls us) often are unable to locate a place in soci-ety where we feel like we belong and have status once we actually do manage to relinquish our institutional life. Thus retirement just comes to mean obscurity and being engaged in meaningless activities to keep us occupied so that we are not perceived as competition for the younger work force. Seniors often confess that they feel shunted aside, useless, replaced as their institutional connections disappear. This emotional state more often than not creates crotchety and stub-born older men and women. Ever met one of these? (My HOA is full of them!) When this occurs, we can be so unpleasant and difficult to deal with as seniors, earning us the reputation of being cranky. The key task for those of us headed into our Wisdom Years becomes one of determining a new identity for ourselves. This is no small project.

And finally, *sadness* infiltrates the senior world because an inher-ent depression comes with aging since death is the inevitable outcome for us and our beloved. Losing our youth is not easy, especially in American culture, and particularly for Baby Boomers who somehow bought into the idea that we would always be youthful, active, beautiful, and immortal. Reality is different, isn't it? Our mortality begins to gnaw at the farthest corner of the brain and increases with intensity each passing year. Every trip to the physician's office adds to the reality that we have fewer years ahead than we have behind us. Depression and alcoholism are two of the most insidious plagues among seniors, according to AARP. These are so often caused by the tragic realities of aging, even when life could be more fulfilling.

And I must mention suicide. Senior suicides are highest among white males, often due to loss of meaning in life, or loss of connection to a mate or friends. This book intends to address this issue in a direct way: Life in the senior years *can* be meaningful and purposeful, but we must intentionally *choose* our life, which demands our courage and new perspectives. Perhaps more in these years than at any other time of life, we are called to *be brave* and *intentional* when fighting even our most demanding demons.

To borrow from Fr. Richard Rohr again, as we move into the Wisdom Years, we are invited to step over the line from *institutional life* to *intentional life*. While this sounds idyllic in practice, for far too many seniors retirement appears as a negative process. For instance, some seniors are forced by their company or organization to retire too early. This situation has happened to several of my friends who were forced, after successful years in careers they valued, to take early retirement or be fired. None were emotionally or mentally ready for retirement, nor were their financial packages in place for this transition. Yet all found, once back in the job market, that they were too old to be reemployed in their respective fields. Being *forced* to retire places a weight on the bonus years that makes younger retirees feel as if being unemployed is more of a burden than a bonus. How *do* we reinvent ourselves when we have to retire before we are ready?

Several of my professional colleagues have a much different situation. They accepted a lucrative early retirement package so the way could be cleared for younger workers to come on the scene. These persons were not required to leave their careers but were *seduced* to retire. Most accepted this option because if they had waited to retire on schedule, the package would be less generous. This creates the awkward situation of retirement coming too many years too early, when almost-seniors are not yet quite finished with their careers. Although these retirees are now financially set, I notice in these folks a sense of incompleteness and agitation as they search for something to do to fill the long daily hours while their friends and spouses are still at work. Feeling somewhat uneasy in their retirement because they believe they should be grateful for their retirement bonus, they are actually unsure about what to do with this early freedom. What began as something quite positive becomes a problem to solve.

Likewise, there is no way to escape the reality that many seniors are thrust into retirement by health issues. Loss of good health can come into play too easily in our bonus years, stealing all the dreams we had for travel and new interests. Dare I say this: Health is probably the single most important aspect to a quality second half of life. I spotted a billboard in Albuquerque recently that reads, "Healthy is Wealthy." I wholeheartedly agree! While finances do matter such that living in poverty as a senior requires stamina many of us cannot imagine, health complications can keep a senior homebound and in a state of both physical and mental suffering. Living with poor health and its complications requires tenacity beyond what seems feasible or possible. Good health fosters the literal "fountain of youth" sought by so many retirees, though this reality is not always present for some.

And perhaps one of the worst ways to be pushed into retirement comes with death or divorce of a spouse close to the senior years. This scenario most often happens to women who have relied on their partner's companionship and income for most of their lives. (This reality commonly marks a certain generation of women who are typically above sixty years of age.) I can also name several male friends for whom being "forced into singleness" by death of his spouse has been devastating, leaving them very lonely and isolated. For so many, the loss of a spouse creates financial or emotional chaos, or both.

Involuntary retirement can manifest a variety of negative scenarios such as being required to start a new job late in life, moving out of one's cherished home, losing financial security, or becoming a nomad by moving from one child to another. More than one story of a retired single person in one of these situations has crossed my doorway.

For those of you familiar with the television series *Doc Martin*, one particular episode tells a poignant story about the death of Doc's father. This leaves his mother with no place to go, so she shows up at the Doc's front door seeking asylum from her dreary life. Her expectation is that the Doc will take her in and care for her, ignoring the fact that her son has a new wife and baby. The ramifications are dramatic and complicated, not ending well for anyone. Usually retirement is painted as the dream vacation of a lifetime with sunny beaches, neighborhood barbecues, romantic travel in Italy, or grandchildren and Disney World. But in far too many situations the opposite becomes the case in point. Again, I ask, "*Who mentors us into our retirement? What will teach us how to face the vicissitudes of aging? How are we to face all the trauma that is possible in our senior years without an adequate guide through this confusing maze of circumstances?*"

Most of us lack preparation when stepping into the *intentional life,* especially if one has been forced into retirement. And even if the move into the senior years is a pleasant experience, complete with the retirement party, bonus gift, and best wishes from our colleagues, the shift away from formal work often causes shock that lasts for weeks, months, even years in some cases. I still experience friends of mine who wander around the halls of their life searching for some point of connection to the person they formerly were, missing the mark as each day passes. Retirement lies on their shoulders as an encumbrance rather than a recently discovered freedom.

I recollect a friend who sold his successful company with a great deal of enthusiasm and glee, then walked out the door into his new life. But within months he was miserable. So he renegotiated with the new CEO a way to consult for his former company. Within two years, both parties were unhappy with the arrangement. My friend left the business for the second time and began an intense search for meaning in this new life beyond the institutional world. He attended self-improvement retreats, hiked and climbed exotic mountains to locate a new Self. Within two years he was miserable again, and this time, severe depression set in. This brilliant, warm, affable man faced a dreadful struggle with his retirement years because once he had accomplished everything he had longed to do, he came to realize there was no meaning in any of it. He had not prepared for the process that leaving the institutional life would set in motion inside his traumatized psyche. Retirement is not simply a time of life without formal institutional work. Rather, it is a *new* beginning requiring a *new* identity to interpret *new* experiences for a time in life never before experienced.

Several thorny issues often shape such an unhappy retirement that, in turn, fail to produce the Wisdom Years we desire. There is no secret to what these issues might be. As I list them, you will immediately recognize the truth of the matter. First, many seniors are attached to the idea that the retirement years must focus on *security*, a settling in to easy rhythms of daily living, where situations are familiar, safe, and comfortable. This usually means having enough money to keep our lives similar to that of our career years, the stamina to exercise and live a physically active life, enough free time to engage in activities we have long wished to do, and the gift of inspiration to follow the path of a heart-felt passion. Yet in this "second half of life," the pull of gravity on the body, mind, and spirit can cause us to settle down into highly routinized days, with little that challenges our minds or bodies. One day begins to look much like another.

Now this is not unpleasant for many folks. In fact, perhaps it feels good to sleep in a bit, have a late breakfast, run to the golf course or gym for a workout, have lunch with a friend, do an errand or two, imbibe a six o'clock cocktail, and then turn to sofa and television for the evening, or attend a concert, depending upon your lifestyle. But the tendency toward routine, even if this includes taking numerous exotic cruises, becomes stronger with each passing day. (I know a couple who take at least four cruises a year. But when asked what these trips accomplish for them, they are simply seeking distraction from the boredom of the endless freedom of retirement living.)

The desire for security—for sameness, habit, uncomplicated days—tends to become more tempting as we age, and risk seems to be what we should avoid. Yet to live for security will bring a slow, sure death to the vitality and adventure of the retirement years. To become too comfortable in that easy chair, in that circle of friends, in that book study club, in that neighborhood bridge circle, out on that golf course, on that deck chair slowly begins to kill the brain cells, to close down the heart and stiffen the body. The next thing we know, when we settle for comfort and security, we find that we are suddenly old and the sparkle has faded from our eyes. Desperation sets in to take that exotic trip, or remodel the kitchen, or purchase a new car, go live in an ashram—anything to make life exciting again. I've seen people conjure a wide variety of possibilities while searching for the one magic bullet that will cause retirement to be as much fun as it is touted to be. This false busyness, in turn, creates a rather frantic lifestyle. I've seen other retirees lapse into such a sedentary daily life, with little to engage the mind and heart, that they seem to decay right before my eyes. The appetite for security can haunt seniors like a vicious dog. To nullify this tendency we must *pay attention and deliberately challenge our stasis.*

A second characteristic of aging that creates complications for our senior years is a prolific *resistance to change.* This behavior follows closely on the security fixation, in that to feel secure, we naturally tend to resist change. But the reality of change is perhaps the most consistent component to a high-quality retirement life. The reason? The senior years are nothing but change! Our bodies are changing almost on a daily basis—just check your bathroom mirror! Our minds are slowing down, even if you do manage to master those online mind games or crossword puzzles on a daily basis. The brain slows in its ability to retrieve previously known data whether we like it or not. The heart falls into apathy as we lose relationships and repeatedly face the death of friends and family members. Our spiritual life languishes unless it is nurtured, which so often seniors forget to do. *Change is the operative word for the aging process.* If we resist this reality, trouble is ahead. The senior years actually demand that we become comfortable with change just at a time when our tendency is to avoid facing the changes in our routines, our bodies, our finances, our homes, our relationships.

Third, a feeling of *vulnerability* can plague us as we age that is unlike any other in our lives, even the teen years. For myself, I notice seniors becoming more conservative in their later years, and I am not speaking particularly of politics, though this is also part of the puzzle of aging. Conservative in this setting means an unwillingness to relinquish our attachment to familiarity. A tendency to halt going out at night or in bad weather begins to creep into lifestyle decisions. We take the elevator instead of walking the stairs. We become less willing to venture across town to attend a lecture we wanted to hear because of the traffic. Sometimes we beef up the security systems in our homes because we become afraid of break-ins. We buy more, not less insurance. Guarding our money and our health as if both will last forever becomes an unconscious desire.

Most seniors soon notice the tendency when we are with friends to discuss our health and well-being before any other topic has a chance to arise. A litany of ailments and doctor's appointments begins to unfold, and a more vital conversation is put on the back burner until everyone has had a chance to unload their health stories. Conversation begins with, "Well, I had to see my doc this week about my hip replacement." Or "I have my second cataract surgery scheduled next week and then I should be able to see again!" Or "I am so tired of these dang growths on my bald head. What's that about anyway?"

After a while, such conversations become almost pathetic or laughable. But at another level this chatter is highly revealing of the feeling of vulnerability that incessantly invades the psyche and body of seniors. Everything from our finances, to our health, to government benefits, to concern over our children or grandchildren, to local politics fosters anxiety and worry. One of the most common statements among "the Elderlies" is this one: "Aging isn't for sissies!" This statement, while humorous, is also a confession about the disabling aspects of aging that leave us feeling raw and vulnerable.

To be willing to be vulnerable as we age is quite contrary to our instincts! We already feel vulnerable because our body is wearing out; our eyesight requires glasses or surgery; we need hearing aids or we shout a lot. We need a knee replaced or a stent put in. And the number of prescriptions that fill our bathroom cabinets proliferates overnight! So to ask us to accept vulnerability as an enlightened state of being rather than as a frailty seems absolutely senseless. Yet our Wisdom Years invite us to live toward change and adaptation, calling us to open our hearts and minds beyond the unconscious abandonment of our younger years. To be vulnerable calls us to receptivity, kindness, patience, gentleness—the virtues of wisdom.

Finally, *fear* can completely absorb the aging years, often without our recognizing this demon of the soul. For some strange reason when we retire from the institutional world, are no longer raising children, and feel the limitations of time, we so often find ourselves plagued with fears. I call this, "I'm feeling left out of the game of life" panic that sets in once we realize we no longer have legitimate or recognized influence in shaping the world around us. A friend recently shared this feeling with my spouse as he told the story of going on vacation with his children. The younger adults and grandchildren all wanted to do activities and have conversations that did not easily include the older adults. The generation gap was alive and well, leading to a vacation that was not particularly satisfactory for the seniors.

I remember quite clearly the moment in my sixties when I realized, "None of this is ever going to become better or easier again!" Aging simply keeps on happening until the end of it all, which is death. A deep "gut fear" sets in and begins to infiltrate our actions, thoughts and even feelings. And all those nagging questions begin to arise: *Who will take care of me when the time comes? Will I lose my mind or body first? How will I die? Will my death be painful?*

Perhaps the most pervasive fear of the senior years is the unspoken fear of a future without us in it. How will I be remembered? How can this possibly happen to *me?* Such questions start out in our forties as a quiet voice, which we simply push aside. (At the first inkling of this reality, my spouse recommends adults read *The Denial of Death* by Ernest Becker.) In our fifties, the reality of our mortality begins to insert itself into our consciousness because our body demands this of us. By the time we are sixty, the death questions are a dull roar pounding in our head, and by age seventy, they blatantly stare us in the face. By the eighties, we just feel lucky to be here at all! (So says my spouse who is eighty-four.) Avoidance of reality at some point along this spectrum of time is no longer an available option. (I have a ninety-six-year-old friend who recently said rather pensively, "I think I better start thinking about death, don't you think so?")

One of the more important books currently available concerning the traumatic realities of aging, nursing homes and dying is *Being Mortal* written by Dr. Atul Gawande. On the NY Times Bestseller list for months on end, this book has struck a profound chord in the psyche of America's aging Boomers. Dr. Gawande makes this statement early in his book, "Our reverence for independence takes no account of the reality of what happens in life: Sooner or later, independence will become impossible. Serious illness or infirmity will strike. It is as inevitable as sunset." Here is where we learn whether we are courageous or not.

With this heavy-duty list of what can go wrong scenarios, you might wonder where this book in your hands will take us—is any decent response possible?

Yes. There are also millions of Baby Boomers whose shift into their senior years has been a positive experience. There *is* the other type of retirement, the one where things are planned out and go smoothly. To address the best of it: we choose our retirement date, complete with financial package and health intact, and we announce our desire to *stop* doing what we had been doing for a chance to *start* a new journey of doing what we wish. Whichever way you see retirement coming at you, the shift is physical in its initial manifestation: We pack up our personal box and walk out into a new reality. There is an actual movement from one place to another. But as we've seen, this physical shift, just like the retirement experience itself, can be stressful, often accompanied by mental, emotional, and even spiritual changes in our lives, regardless of whether retiring has been a pleasurable experience or not.

Now that I have you positively alarmed about the aging process, I want to encourage you to read the remainder of the book. This book is NOT depressing! This book concerns *the antidote* to the exigencies of aging that can leave us angry or depressed, worried or anxious. There actually is a way to live the *intentional life* with purpose, joy, meaning, determination, and courage. Robert Love, Editor in Chief of the AARP magazine wrote, "Sad that the f-word (fun) never gets used much when talking about aging." He is right. Fun is a difficult word to apply to the tough realities of aging. But we should apply the word, nonetheless. Aging *can* be fun if we can break our addiction to our former lives and approach these senior days with intention, purpose, meaning, and delight. This book is about how to give this perspective a try.

The quote at the beginning of this chapter by David Whyte states my intention for this book:

"Someone has written something new in the ashes of your life."

That someone is you. *YOU* may, if you choose, write a new story into the ashes of the institutional life you are leaving behind for your newly found Wisdom Years. Just as Fr. Rohr stated, "No one can keep you from the second half of your own life except yourself." If we allow ourselves to wallow in the negative aspects of the "aging trap," there is plenty to discourage us. I learned when I set my mind to exploring this quandary that while we are not in charge of the *quantity* of our senior years, we can certainly take charge of the *quality* of our "second half of life." If we set about challenging those annoying quirks and realities of aging with intention and determination, we can change the tone and timbre of our days, our activities, our living. The end, we cannot control—we will die. But since the outcome is that predictable, don't the days between now and then matter? I believe they do.

Living into the Wisdom Years with zest, energy, excitement, adventure is my intention in this book. If this is your goal, keep reading and I will share with you what I did to break into this mode of living in my own life, to step across the line from institutional life to intentional life and on into the Wisdom Years. I did this by designing four pilgrimages for myself the year I turned seventy as a way to engage stepping across that invisible retirement line. I purposefully designed each one with a different goal and intention to awaken myself to this precarious aging project that my life has handed me. What is the gift for me in this exercise of aging? Walking. I have become a walker. This is my new calling. Thich Nhat Han teaches us to "walk like me" in a documentary film about his meditative life style. After viewing this film, I recognized that my choice to become a walker is more about mindfulness, meditation, and nurturing a new spiritual depth than it is about pleasure or exercise. Walking creates for me the motion, movement, and motivation for wisdom to engage my body, soul, and mind.

The rest of this book reveals my journeys, the insights I gained and how all of this changed my life so that I am *not* living as a retiree, but as a person who is joyfully exploring the intentional life. (Thank you, Fr. Rohr!)

Chapter 2:
The Courage to Climb
Pilgrimage No. 1: Exterior Story

"I care less and less about more and more,
yet the things I do care about take
me deeper and deeper into my soul."
—Skye Boyd

I pen the epigram to this chapter in my journal on the third day of my first walking/hiking pilgrimage. This journey of the body takes me into the Superstition Mountains of Arizona outside of Phoenix for the first half of my venture and then on to Chaco Canyon in northwestern New Mexico for the final days. The drive from Santa Fe to our destination includes a spontaneous stop in Pie Town, New Mexico, to check out whether the myths about this place and its delicious pies are true. Cleve and I are charmed by the idea of a village off the beaten path that exists solely to serve a variety of sumptuous desserts to the thousands who travel here merely for a taste of these savory delights. I have now checked Pie Town off my "bucket list."

As the car hums along the back roads of the Land of Enchantment, Cleve entertains me with stories of his childhood growing up in Colorado. This is the first time I realize that this man can easily pass for an authentic cowboy. My first pilgrimage companion may turn out to be more than I bargained for!

My *compadre* and I arrive in Lost Dutchman State Park in the late afternoon, tired, hungry, and ready to pitch our respective tents. The month is April. If you know anything about this part of the country—

the Southwest—by this time of the year the days are already beginning to be too warm and the nights can still drop below freezing.

I watch the expertise with which Cleve sets his tent; it looks comfortable and inviting with its spaciousness and thick sleeping pad. My tent goes up easily enough, but it's smaller in size and the thinner sleeping pad I chose with pride when I packed my gear will come back to haunt me. I suffer for this choice over the next eight days with a sore back and aching hips. But such as it is, this cozy tent becomes my "home on the desert," and I am committed to just being here in this place, in this moment.

Cleve and I fall into our tents without dinner that first night, expecting to experience the sleep of the dead. Soon I hear soft snoring sounds coming from his tent. I shudder in my sleeping bag as uneasiness afflicts me in the pitch-black darkness that swallows me. The night fills with an eerie cacophony: coyotes howling in the distance, evening birds chirping, red-eye flights of airplanes overhead flying from Los Angeles to New York City, creepy rustling in the shrubbery, the skittering sounds of nocturnal creatures across the sand (Arizona desert scorpion?) an incessant wind flapping my tent. How in the world can the desert *be* so noisy? I grumble, yanking the sleeping bag flap over my head to drown out the sounds. I am restless much of the night, sleeping only fitfully. Waking tired and cranky the next morning, I crave hot food, water and a way to escape the already beaming sun.

Once we have downed our breakfast and cleaned the campsite, Cleve and I head into some of the most imposing mountains I have ever explored, to locate just the perfect spot for viewing and photographing Weaver's Needle. The hike up Fremont Pass is long and sweaty, arduous actually. Jumbled rocks and ruts do not offer an easy climb, even for veteran hikers like us. To keep my energy intact and my feet focused on the goal, my eyes constantly search for the saddle between the two ridges ahead of us. At random intervals, Cleve and I turn around to peer down into the desert floor we have left behind, the trail behind us winding down the rugged mountainside like a rattlesnake in motion. We slug water in gulps and gasps to quench our thirst.

Out of breath and with legs aching, we eventually arrive at the top of a boulder-cluttered bluff and plop ourselves down on cool stones under the brow of a shaded mesa wall. The scenery in these mountains takes my breath away as I stare over the ridges and edges of ragged cliffs toward the Needle. Surely the Universe was having a party when all of this beauty came into being! My stomach soon urges me to turn my attention away from the vistas before me to my own immediate need for sustenance. Time for that smashed PBJ sandwich and the apple I have been craving for the last mile of the hike. A drink from the lukewarm water in my bottle, a few photos on my phone, and once more, I glance around at the formations protruding into the cloudless skies above. I sigh with contentment as my eyelids grow heavy, and I slip into a much-needed, lazy catnap. What a perfect day!

After we rouse from our snooze, Cleve leaves his perch and vanishes across the ridge. I am fine—for a while. Then the sky, which has surreptitiously filled with billowy clouds, begins to make rumbling noises that I easily recognize. The afternoon mountain showers are looming. For a while I sit perplexed, wondering whether to go hunt for my friend, hunker under a rock, or head back down the trail. Time passes excruciatingly slowly and no Cleve. Sprinkles begin to turn into large drops, washing the dust off the rocks and shrubbery. The decision is made for me. Scurrying for cover into a clump of imposing boulders, I hide in the crevices away from the rain. Hurriedly digging a waterproof poncho out of my pack, I crouch down to wait out the storm. Like most of these afternoon showers, the skies clear again before long, leaving traces of dampness on the bushes around me. I slowly emerge from my improvised cave. Still no Cleve. My heart begins to pound with anxiety. What if he has fallen and is injured? Should I try to find him? Should I just wait for him to return and risk being caught on the side of this mountain in the dark? Should I head back down to camp? Do I need to go for help?

Just as I am about to engage in a full-blown panic attack, there he is! Grinning like a Cheshire cat, arriving on time as he had promised. Unaware of my discomfort, he chatters about his adventure to locate a hidden place on the ledge above our heads that he had wanted to find, a memory from hiking in this area with some college buddies. I don't know whether to be mad or embarrassed, so I say nothing and begin a stoic march behind him back down the mountain to our campsite. Later that night in my tent, I spend some time monitoring my own reactions to this experience. There had been absolutely no reason for me to become afraid sitting among those boulders. I have been in this situation on more than one occasion after years of hiking and backpacking. Cleve had promised me he would return at a certain time and he did. An important lesson is brewing inside me to be added to others that are already piling up in my mind and journal as I log this pilgrimage. Is this new "fear" because I am older now and feel more vulnerable when left alone on a mountaintop? Is this a new aging reality? The need for courage plants its first seeds in my heart. "I have such a long way to go," I mumble as I fall asleep.

The next day we are both up early for a nature hike among some of the most unusual cactus plants I have ever seen. Mesmerized by their various shapes, sizes and colors, I gasp at the beauty of it all. Huge saguaros tower over the landscape like headless men. Barrel cacti are fastened to the ground like stumps, and cactus trees with odd pieces of froth hanging from them decorate the brown desert floor. Flowers perched on the various prickly plants look like beautiful butterflies coming home to roost. The sounds of desert birds fill the air constantly as if they are all talking to each other. Even the rocks are covered with multicolored striations. I satisfy my astonishment by taking one photo after another on my phone.

During the daylight hours, my friend and I have to hide from the white blaze of the heat, but evenings bring coolness back into the air and the chance to head out once again into the desert to witness its dusky magic. After a delicious camp-food supper, Cleve and I stroll through the sand staring at the plants, listening to the chirping of the desert birds, admiring the distant glowing horizon that has become available to us as the sun drops below the peaked mountains. I sigh with elation. I am at my best when I am out of doors, for sure.

I am a desert person. I was reared among the sands, cacti and tumbleweeds in the Panhandle of West Texas. So I have long loved the stark, flat landscapes with their scorching, sunny days and starry,

starry nights. The dust storms out here are rare but fierce when they happen. Sunsets are spectacular, a canvas of color that even Georgia O'Keeffe would struggle to paint. I feel so at home in the desert that a gentle stillness fills the depths of my soul. It's been a long time since I have known such quiet peace.

Each day offers this predictable rhythm: devouring my hearty oatmeal breakfast, intense hikes in the heat, seeking the canyons and crevices of the mountains to eat lunch and rest, and then a return to camp, tired and hot, for a sumptuous dinner (thanks to the chef-like skills of my hiking partner). Once the last dish has been washed and put away, we head for our camp chairs to relax and read—and to wait for the lightshow to begin. The ravishing sunsets on this desert are nothing short of glorious sky-paintings sprung from such brilliant colors as to make my eyes water with tears from sheer joy at the sight.

Following these rituals, we stare at the heavens as the sunset fades and the first star peeps out. Cleve and I sit contentedly under the most splendid twinkling light-spackled night skies I have ever seen. A simple conversation passes between us about plans for the next day, and then we fall into silence. The day is done and permission is mutually granted to withdraw. Cleve pours his nightly glass of whiskey and begins to slowly sip the amber drink, lost in thought.

I take to my tent to continue reading Rev. Barbara Brown Taylor's book, *Leaving Church*, a book I can easily say begins to relieve my wounded soul of one of its heaviest burdens: how to leave the church (and my ordination) with lessened guilt. How do I break the spell of attachment to my career and relinquish my institutional service years to create the longed-for intentional years of purpose and meaning? This question lingers in my mind as I fall asleep.

Halfway through this first pilgrimage, we pack up the car and head north into the mountains to camp in the coolness of the forests away from the desert heat. This venture quickly becomes a joke! As Cleve drives higher and higher into the Tonto National Forest, the roads become muddy with deep ruts in them. "What is that white stuff on the ground?" I ask like a fool. Cleve, who has a very droll sense of humor, looks over his sunglasses at me and says one word: "Snow," drawing the word out like a piece of stretched taffy. I become uncomfortably quiet. I have not prepared to camp in the snow. My tent is too light, my clothing is not appropriate, and I do not have the proper gear for snow camping.

After another few bumpy miles pass by, I dare to respond, "I don't think I can do this—camp in the snow." I wait for him to become grouchy about this statement since he has driven so far at this point, but Cleve simply nods, turns the car around and heads back to a little town called Payson, Arizona. There we clamor out of the car without speaking, shuffle into separate rooms in a two-star motel and give ourselves some time to regroup. Finally, after a cheap, faux Italian dinner in a local diner calms both of us, we return to our respective rooms for the rest of the evening without negotiating our expectations for the next day. Now please allow me to backtrack a bit.

Preparing to take this first pilgrimage, I spent several weeks wondering about the person I could invite to be my guide and guest on the trip. I pondered several of my female friends who hike and camp, but all of them are employed and could not leave their work. Mentally rummaging through my friend list, I finally decided that a compatible, retired friend from Colorado with whom I have canoed and camped for years would be a perfect person to join me on this weird "pilgrimage for aging thingy." I texted Cleve explaining that I wanted to do a pilgrimage to push myself, testing whether I was still capable of hiking and camping at my age. I wondered if he would join me. He graciously responded in the affirmative, and we began planning our trip. Cleve had been one of my parishioners in the church I served in Aurora, Colorado. I have always appreciated and respected his natural way of being in the world. He's a straightforward man, a Colorado cowboy/hunter/wilderness guy with a terrific sense of humor, a sharp tongue, a quick mind, well read and intelligent. His "soft spot" is his wife and daughter, but other than this, he's a man's man, pragmatic and stable.

So knowing this about Cleve, when the two of us part and head to our rooms for the night without negotiating our next day, I feel some sense of trepidation. I fear he will want to cancel the rest of the trip, thinking this venture has been a waste of his time. However, it isn't long before a hot shower and the deeply-mattressed bed puts my worries out of my mind for the time being. I sleep soundly.

The delight in being good friends is often that synchronistic events occur, needing no explanation. The next morning, as we exit our rooms and meet in the hallway to go to breakfast in the dining hall, Cleve and I look at each other and almost simultaneously say, "How about Chaco Canyon?" Cleve nods agreement, and I sigh in relief. After a nondescript meal of limp eggs and bland toast, we are soon back in the car for the long drive into northwestern New Mexico and the ancient Pueblo ruins of the immense Chaco landscapes. Expecting more desert-like conditions similar to where we have been in Arizona, we find ourselves surprised when we begin to set camp and throw up our tents in the rain. Staking my tent in the wet sand gives me pause as I wonder if it will hold in place through the night. Before long, we dive into our shelters to escape the dampness. The night is beyond chilly as I huddle down into my sleeping bag, hoping against reality to stay warm.

Waking to a cold and cloudy day, Cleve and I push through our usual morning routine with our camp kitchen. By this time in the pilgrimage, we have become familiar enough with each other to create patterns that work for each of us and make us efficient at our chores. Dishes washed and daypacks loaded, we set off to hike through some of the ruins of the Chaco complex. Grassy plains and mesa walls became home to several pueblo sites, all crumbling into obscurity as the tracks of humans who lived here so long ago form a story that we can only guess at now.

We spend our first day here scouting the Canyon area. Cleve comments occasionally as we take in the history, the landscapes, the expansiveness of it all. Our first hike takes us to the leaning walls of a former pueblo home. Around the corner from this site we find petroglyphs on some massive boulders high above us. After locating the ancient symbols on the red rock walls, Cleve and I move down the road to tour the grandness of Pueblo Bonito, the key site most people come to view in Chaco Canyon. These experiences grant me the chance to acknowledge how holy this place truly is. No wonder people who come to Chaco feel a reverence for it and want it protected.

A couple of hours pass and we stroll back to the car to drive on to Fajada Butte, so we can stare at this natural phenomenon pasted against the horizon of a crisp, blue sky. The site is actually postcard stunning, almost unbelievable. Rising impressively out of the flatness of the plains, the Butte dares us to capture this sight with our cameras. After several moments of taking more photos than necessary of the Butte, we drive around several of the paved loops, viewing more pueblo ruins. The drive is surreal, as if I have stepped back in time a thousand years. I can almost hear children playing among the walls that are left standing. I imagine brown-skinned women carrying baskets loaded with food, as the men stretch skins across wooden lattices or sit crouched together around a small fire. The sounds of human life waft across the desert from that time long ago. I feel a shiver run up my spine even though the day is now warm. We drive away from this area as a practical question hovers in my head: "How did these Ancient Peoples find enough water to live here in this vast openness?"

The sun begins to wane as Cleve and I return to our camp for the evening's meal, to ponder the day's hikes and settle into our camp chairs for reading. We both love to read, so we slip into an easy silence as each of us fades into our books. At this point, I am immersed in Edward Abbey's *Desert Solitaire* at Cleve's recommendation. Abbey's brilliant descriptions of the desert so completely absorb my mind, as if I am actually traveling with him through the colorful Canyonlands of Utah. Completely engrossed in my book, I fail to notice time leaping forward.

Before long a magnificent sunset begins to splash itself across the high mesa walls that are the backdrop for our tents. Vivid reds and yellows blind us with their brightness. Could anything *be* more beautiful than this? The temperature begins to drop so I don my favorite flannel-lined camping jacket as the night air chills us. Our campfire conversation is lighthearted but subdued while Cleve sips slowly from his metal cup. In a land this huge, I feel as if I am in a cathedral, and that our talk should be held to whispers. One can feel and hear the spirits of long-ago people and their stories in this place. The first star soon pops out as if it intends to be noticed, commanding our attention. This park in which we are camping is a "dark night sky" park, which means that with no mechanical lighting to disturb the landscape, the night sky is so close that we can almost feel it settle around our shoulders like a soft, woolen wrap. Here we are in sacred land, for sure!

One final story before we turn east for Santa Fe. The night before our last day in Chaco is one of the coldest nights I have ever known on a camping trip. I simply could not get warm. My tent and clothing are totally inadequate to the temperature in the desert, and I am miserable all night, as I squirm and wiggle to create heat in my sleeping bag. A frost settles over the campsite and my tent as the temperatures plunge throughout the night. "What in the world was I thinking?" Coming out here without the proper gear? Sleep eludes me.

The only rescue for this nighttime fiasco is the upcoming day's anticipated adventure. This thought assuages the stiffness in my body as I rise slowly from the exhausting night where time moved at a crawl. I thought the morning would *never* come! This final day in Chaco frames the pinnacle of the journey for me—the reason for this particular pilgrimage, though I only realize this later in retrospect. Cleve and I rise early because he wants to climb the mesa wall behind Pueblo Bonito in order to be on top of the mesa and look down over the ruins from that height.

At the beginning of our journey together I had granted Cleve the unspoken right to select our trails and hikes, so I follow him blithely to the beginning point of the trailhead rising steeply up the mesa wall through a very narrow crevice. Never once do I suspect what would be required to get to the top. I assume there will be a switch-back dirt trail all the way up. But as we arrive at the entrance to the trail, I gasp. I don't *do* heights! They terrify me, and with a touch of vertigo, climbing rock walls seems entirely too much for my brain to accept as normal activity. And this trail begins with an almost vertical climb up 130 feet! The "trail" is actually not a trail, but a demanding climb through a crevice created by a piece of the high wall separated, though still standing, from the mesa itself. Large stones and boulders have cascaded into the space between the two sections of wall, creating a rugged pathway that requires climbing and crawling (no walking possible) up to the top of the mesa. Just looking at the situation is daunting. My body freezes as I realize my fearless guide expects me to do this with him. Cleve starts his climb like a lizard, one foot on one stone, the other foot reaching for his next step on the wall. He shinnies up without a moment's hesitation, quickly gaining ground ahead of me.

I suck in my breathe, and start the climb, refusing to look down, but all the while mumbling under my breath, "I may get up here eventually but who is going to bring in the helicopter to take me down off this mesa?" Having short legs and a small body, I have to pull myself up through the rock crevices with sheer strength of will, one foot at a time seeking a toehold. I pray harder than I have prayed in a long time. Falling would be excruciating, so this is *not* an option. Bit by bit, I make my way, one handhold at a time, placing my feet carefully, pulling my body weight forward as I press my back against the rock wall. Time seems to stand still, and the climb to the mesa top seems endless. This is *not* fun, my body screams. Will I *ever* get there?

With sheer will and adrenalin pouring wildly through my limbs, I finally make it! As I manage to toss myself onto the mesa floor, I am panting hard. My emotions are mixed: half angry at Cleve for insisting on the climb, and half excited that I accepted his challenge and conquered my fear of heights—at least for this one time. The spectacular 360-degree view claims my attention immediately, erasing my previous emotions. No wonder this is called "the God's eye" view!

Pueblo Bonito—meaning "beautiful village"—had belonged to the Anasazi peoples hundreds of years ago and is spread out below us in splendor. The earthen rooms and round kivas reveal a small town created in an orderly, semicircular fashion, carefully cast upon the plains. The walls of the remaining structures are formed with stone masonry that still stands regally against the bluest skies you can imagine. From this vantage point I feel as if I am a hawk circling around the images of human habitation down below. As I focus my attention on the patterns of the Pueblo, my mind fills with questions about the stories that have had their origins in this place. Who were these people and what mattered to them? What would it be like to live in such a lonely, isolated place, yet so close to nature? What were their daily routines? How long were they here? Why did they settle here?

After I have saturated my vision with the remains of civilization below, it strikes me that I am on *top* of a mesa. Surveying my surroundings, I turn around with a jolt and exclaim, "There are more ruins up here!" How in the world is that possible? Cleve and I strike out for a set of crumbling walls over-looking a valley on the far side of the mesa. The hike is not short. As the sun blazes down on our backs, I notice my arms are turning red and that I need sunscreen. Within an hour, I am more than ready to find a shady spot to sit and eat my lunch. My stomach rumbles, demonstrating that breakfast has long disappeared from my digestive system. Climbing that mesa wall burned more calories than I had expected. Finally, Cleve and I locate a shady spot on the side of a pueblo ruin where the sun has not yet penetrated with its scorching tentacles. As I plop down on the ground, I feel the coolness of the mud wall against my back. Rest, food, and water! I never fail to be amazed at how enjoyable hiking nibbles and warm water tastes in these settings. Nuts, an apple, peanut butter crackers, a granola bar, dried fruits. Delicious!

After our brief lunch, Cleve and I spend the afternoon as nascent explorers wandering the top. Following a trail that at times comes dangerously close to the rim of the mesa, we pass up and down heavily trekked hills. Soon we find ourselves walking across hard, flattened, black slabs of rock covered with fossils embedded in the shiny stone. As I bend down to peer at the remains of life from thousands of years ago, I wonder about the geology of this area. At some point in time deep waters covered this mesa. I take photos of one fossil that appears over and over again and then reluctantly begin to follow Cleve who has moved on ahead of me.

As a child and young adult, I often gathered rocks and fossils, consistently curious about the time when they were not made of stone but were living creatures floating as some long-ago living flotsam. The past flashes in my mind as I remember those days of curiosity about the earth and its formation. Two of the earliest college courses that I took were in geology. What happened to that fascination with rocks and fossils that held me captive so long ago? Why do we outgrow such interests, or do they simply fade because we no longer pay attention or wish to explore them? What pulls us on to other intellectual or emotional pursuits as we age? Do these interests return in our later years? I sense one of those "life lessons" coming on as I wander off to follow Cleve.

Hiking to a point on the mesa that overlooks another ruin below, Chetro Ketl appears before me. My eyes feast on the mysterious ruins. There are no words in my vocabulary for this experience. Simply lovely to behold. The two of us stand side by side, staring for a long time at the ancient village below. I look up at Cleve, and he shakes his head in wonderment, then turns without speaking, and begins the hike back to the trailhead. We are returning to the trail that will take us back down the mesa wall. The closer we come to the test ahead, the harder and louder my heart pounds. Fear consumes my mind. How am I going to get down from here?

When we arrive at the point of our descent, Cleve states matter-of-factly, "It will be easier if you go down backward, facing the wall." At this point I am *not* about to follow his instructions. My fear is too great not to watch where I am going. I begin moving down the crevice gingerly, facing outward where I can see what I am doing. It isn't long before I realize I could really get hurt going down over these rocks this way. Cleve is right. If I follow his lead, and turn around for the descent, I can move with more confidence and surer feet, even though I will not be able to see what I am doing. I will have to *trust* the feel of my feet upon the rocks and my arms to hold me. I slowly turn around and begin the climb down. Sweat breaks out all over my body, though not from the heat. In this instance, time evaporates as I move one foot and then the other in spider-like manner down and over the rocks. Much to my surprise, the climb down literally takes what feels like seconds, nothing like the painstakingly slow amount of time it took to climb to the heights. We have been on the top of the mesa, and then miraculously we are down on the canyon floor, back on the trail.

My astonishment holds me captive for the return trip to our campsite. How in the world did I manage to do that? There's a lesson here that I must attend to later: *How does time function when we are afraid versus when we feel confident? What is the role of trust in our lives as we adapt to living with aging bodies?* I suspect my questions will have something to do with *courage* as I move deeper into this pilgrimage project.

The trip back to Santa Fe occurs without incident. The first pilgrimage is over. My heart and head are swimming with images, insights, inspiration. There are so many thoughts swirling in my mind, so much to reflect upon and consider. In no way have I placed expectations on the pilgrimages to provide me with deep and meaningful experiences. Actually, this is one of my early vows to myself, about all of the pilgrimages I will take throughout the year: to relinquish as many expectations as I am able and simply allow the experiences to be what they will be. I do not want to preprogram this journey or any of the others ahead of me. I simply wish to be open to what happens. And at least for the first pilgrimage, this vow works. I return to Santa Fe in a contemplative place inside myself pleased with the pilgrimage and aware that the interior processing ahead of me will reveal more than I can, at the moment, process. For now, I can say, "I did it!" I complete this first pilgrimage with one particular word on my mind: *peace.*

CHAPTER 3:
THE WALK FOR LIFE
PILGRIMAGE NO. 1: INTERIOR STORY

> The world of imagination and the illusion of fear and hope
> are great obstacles to the pilgrim on the path.
> —Rumi

At this point, perhaps I should define what I mean by the word *pilgrimage* since there can be multiple uses for this word. Pilgrimage is ordinarily employed to denote a religious journey, including rituals, to a sacred site for devotional reasons. Some pilgrimages you may have heard of, such as travel to Jerusalem, Mecca, Santiago, even Lourdes. While these are all pilgrimages couched in the Abrahamic faiths, there are well-known pilgrimages, such as the Kumbh Mela in India, that belong to Eastern religions. Even Shinto believers in Japan and Buddhists around the world have pilgrimage rituals. I am, however, in this book using the word pilgrimage in a more secular and/or spiritual manner rather than as a religious definition. Though my four pilgrimages do lead me to psychological and spiritual conclusions, which come full circle in the last chapter of this book, I did not set out on this project to discover for myself either religious connections or their consequences. Thus, I would like for you to consider this definition (my own) as you read my story:

Pilgrimage *is an intentional journey that requires one to leave home and walk (or travel) to some chosen destination with the distinct purpose to nurture psychological, mental, emotional, and/or spiritual growth that creates a change in actions, behaviors, and worldview on the part of the pilgrim.*

I offer this understanding of pilgrimage because this type of journey is not simply travel merely for the sake of going somewhere. Nor is pilgrimage a hiking trek or vacation. Likewise, for many pilgrims, these experiences are not designed to be religious or even spiritual journeys. My pilgrimages fall into this category, for instance. Interpreting the definition above, a pilgrimage has two critical aspects to it: an *exterior* experience, usually arduous in some way, that includes leaving home, and an *interior* intention or purpose designed to create transformation within, returning the pilgrim home again with a new sense of Self. One cannot accidentally take a pilgrimage! The pilgrim *intentionally* and *deliberately* designs and prepares for the pilgrimage with the sole purpose of *change* occurring for her or him. My time with Cleve in the Superstition Mountains and Chaco Canyon as shared in the previous chapter became the exterior report of the first pilgrimage I intentionally designed.

I first want you to know that the exterior pilgrimage that I took with Cleve lasted ten days, from driving out of Santa Fe to my return home. So why didn't I expressly share with you each day of the trip west? Because that would have turned my pilgrimage story into a travel memoir. I shared with you the particular experiences, both physical and emotional, that deeply affected me, whether positively or negatively, demanding that I face and change certain aspects of my self-understanding. Cleve and I actually took several other hikes and car trips than those I have disclosed to you. Although these ventures were delightful in their own way, nothing of particular consequence occurred on those days that put me under pressure to scrutinize them for interior growth. Overall, the experiences from this first pilgrimage renewed my spirit and body and were more than exhilarating. But for the purpose of opening myself to you in light of the journey into my Wisdom Years, I logged the specific moments that tested me in some important way, expanding my personal horizons.

Now I wish to stop at this point, share a rather painful story with you, and define for you what I mean by our *Wisdom Years*. I actually hope you have noticed my use of this term and have begun to wonder what it means for this book. The idea for the words "Wisdom Years" came to me during my sixtieth birthday year when I traveled in Ireland with a group of female friends. (Are you beginning to notice a pattern here? Yes, I have planned and executed a substantial ritual each birthday year decade beginning with my fortieth year.) Turning sixty for this Baby Boomer was daunting, to say the least. So without sufficient awareness at the time, I planned a "croning ritual" with a close female friend to take place in Ireland. I did not fully understand why this ritual seemed important for me to do, just that I should. Later I came to understand the reason for the pilgrimage.

"Crone" can mean malicious woman (most often the use in American parlance). But more pertinent to this story the word "crone" can also mean "wise woman" with magical or healing powers. I designed my ritual around this second interpretation of the word.

The rite of passage ceremony that Carolyn planned for me at St. Brigit's Garden, out of Galway, Ireland, was one of the loveliest experiences in my entire life. Our group of women walked through these Celtic gardens, admiring the landscapes, the art, the shaped ponds, enjoying even the damp and cloudy day. The gardens provided a hospitable welcome thrilling the group as we explored the various scenes created among the grasses, shrubs and flowers. Soon, the time came to gather in the Round House to share the ritual for my birthday and the advent of my Wisdom Years. (Or so I believed!) Exchanging personally made gifts and listening to the thrum of Celtic music, we chanted and sang together, honoring the feminine spirit in all of us. The rite lasted for about an hour and was a true blessing of women's energy as we shared what it meant to join the ranks of the wise mentors in our lives.

The "croning" ritual was accomplished. Supposedly now I could be named among the wise women of my world! Holding our umbrellas to shelter us against the light drizzle that was falling, the group made its way to the dining room with subdued conversations occurring here and there. I walked alone, lagging behind, deep in thought.

We were honored with a lovely luncheon planned by one of Carolyn's Irish friends and spiritual teachers. The day bespoke a splendid marking to the beginning of my Wisdom Years. Except it wasn't!

Underneath all the ritual blessings, what I felt was a mixture of emotions. At one level I felt excited and humbled by the ceremony I had just experienced. At another level I was like a wounded animal wishing I could escape from the group and vanish into thin air. I will explain.

Other than this particular day of the trip, the day of the croning ritual itself, the entire journey became, for me, a fiasco. I had chosen the wrong group of women to join me for my birthday pilgrimage. Quickly it became evident that I had not properly set the tone for the seriousness and spiritual depth of the trip that I had envisioned. I could not make sense of things that were occurring on the trip with some of the women. Friends with whom I had felt close became strangers to me on this journey, acting in ways that totally puzzled and hurt me. When I arrived back in America, I felt alienated and wounded. I broke connections with many in this group of women and never spoke of my "croning" ritual again to any of them. Even my reactions to all of this were not helpful to them or me.

It has taken me a long time to understand what happened on this sixtieth birthday journey. What I finally came to see, as I returned to my normal routine of life, was that I was a long way from being wise. A true crone, a wise woman, would *never* have chosen this particular group of women to go with her on this unique journey. Nor would she have displayed the reactions I did to this event. I had let my ego desire for deeper connections with some of the group override my own sense of personal intention for self-discovery, and I selected persons who were nowhere near that stage of life for themselves. In no way could some of the women, given who they were and what phase of life they were in, have understood what Carolyn and I intended for this ritual. For some of these friends, this venture was a fun vacation trip to Ireland; for others, it was a time for scoping out new relationships. But for me this trip was intended to be a purposeful pilgrimage. I had set myself up for the journey to be an abysmal failure simply because I was not mindful of the group dynamics or personal agendas of the participants. Thus my first lesson in how wisdom actually develops in our souls and minds began to take shape in my sixtieth year of life. I was not yet there for sure!

I began through the decade of my sixties to become more and more aware that wisdom is not a word to use carelessly. First lesson: *Becoming wise is a process that does not begin with a ritual that declares one to be wise.* True wisdom begins with self-knowledge and the ability to be truthful *to* oneself *about* oneself. There is no way to build solid relationships with others until we fully grasp who we are ourselves. Wisdom comes with awareness and humility of self and moves forward to *beingness* and *authenticity* of character and personhood. It's not about words we speak, or actions we take. Wisdom is a way of being in the world, with integrity, awareness, joy, and self-discipline. So this aging process in which I am now involved at almost age seventy demands far more integrity and intelligence than any other decade of my life. In order to age wisely, we first must admit to ourselves our deepest fears and frustrations with aging and yes, our mortality. Only then might wisdom even begin to plant seedlings in our hearts and minds, and behaviors.

I have begun, at age seventy, to view the aging process as a stage play. Life prior to this age is a rehearsal for a one-night play. Now begins the performance, which requires intense awareness and consciousness. Everything from here until my death is "in the moment" of the play, and the play is live! Everything that happens now until my death is the "real deal" because there is no longer time for rehearsal, for practice, for figuring out who I am and what I am supposed to be doing with my life. Now I need to know my lines, be on stage and be alert. The curtain is rising. It's show time!

One of the key insights on my first pilgrimage is quite basic: How do I get all my gear into a backpack, my clothing into a small duffel, and keep my impact on Cleve's car as compact as possible? In other words, the *preparations* for the pilgrimage are just as important as the journey itself. Because Cleve hauled our cooking gear, kitchen tent, ice chests, camp chairs, and various other pieces of equipment we would need to use, it became imperative that I keep my gear small and tidy. Thus the first lesson for engaging the Wisdom Years becomes *simplicity*. One of the critical tasks of the aging years invites us to make our "gear" smaller. In other words, we need to downsize everything. Everything from our houses, to finances, to garages and storage units (yes, seniors have entirely too many storage units!), to personal memoirs, left over clutter from our children, and most importantly, our interior life.

I have heard over and over again the complaints of adult children whose parents or grandparents pass away, leaving them with the task of clearing out Mom and Dad's home lived in for thirty or forty years. What a truly painful "gift" to pass on to our children! So many seniors ignore this issue rather absentmindedly, unaware of what offspring suffer in order to sift and sort through their parents' belongings. Other seniors leave this task to their children deliberately. I often wonder if the parents want their heirs to secretly discover who they really are by going through their belongings and memoirs, or is this a sort of denial of their own impending death?

Whatever the reason, organizing our households, finances and legal matters to make them simpler and easier to manage aids our children or other kin, and in some cases even grandchildren, in a myriad of ways. In my own case, my siblings and I were left struggling to find our parents' will and legal papers upon their unexpected deaths. We knew the documents existed, but Mother and Dad had not told us where the papers were kept. So we started the necessary legal processes in chaos, all the while being in shock and grief. This situation can be easily resolved if seniors will become comfortable with the process of going simple as we age. Let go before we die! Get our papers and physical life in order while we are still healthy, both physically and mentally! Tell our designated survivors where important documents are located (or better yet, give them copies), and make our dying and death a matter of simplicity and grace. Then we can let go of the worry about all of this and live with gusto! Become a playful Wise One! Then, and only then, can our Wisdom Years become a time of creativity, joy, and deliberate intention.

Aging requires us to do all that we can to make our exterior lives simpler and easier to maneuver. Less to take care of, more time for pursuing Wisdom Years goals. But making changes only in our physical lives and keeping our interior lives cluttered does not help much. Does it? The mission to simplify life also has an interior calling. So you ask: How do I unclutter my interior life? Stepping over the line from the institutional life into the intentional life means letting go of attachments to everything from past work habits, regrets and grudges, old painful stories we harbor that corrupt new growth, as well as our persistent inability to accept change. It means letting go of failed life stories, such as my sixtieth birthday year ritual, a previous boss, a troublesome aunt, while intentionally allowing wisdom to begin to find a new home in our minds and bodies. This is the task!

Try to do an assessment of some grudge you are holding against a former colleague at work, or a family member, or neighbor. Do you *really* need to keep that grudge alive and kicking? How well is this serving you? Engage in those conversations that will bring release from such inhibiting attachments. Or simply forgive and move on, dropping the issue entirely. Our Wisdom Years allow us to lighten up our emotional burdens through the actions of forgiveness and reconciliation. An attitude of "how important can this really be?" becomes possible as we age. Pretend you are dying next week: Do you really want the last seven days of your life spent being angry at your Uncle Harry? Most of us would shout a resounding "No!" So live like that *now*. Forgive. Forget. Move on. Lighten your heart and free your mind.

Living the interior life with simplicity can lure us away from the complaints and crankiness of aging into more positive, healthy ways of being. Why *are* so many seniors angry or depressed or just plain grouchy all the time? Have you noticed? While health and medications can certainly play a huge role in this question (and I do not want to make light of this reality for many) for the rest of us the answer lies in *attitude*. Choosing to lighten up your life is not an easy task, I grant you. Simplicity requires the actions of letting go and surrendering, which makes us feel vulnerable. Have you noticed how much better you feel with all your stuff around you, including unhealthy emotions? But if we face the truth of our story, these belongings and emotions cannot go with us when we die. So if we can winnow our excess baggage, both exterior and interior, we begin to become lighter in spirit, heart, and mind. Then, space opens in the psyche for wisdom to enter and nestle there.

So let's ask ourselves some key questions: What weighs you down and makes your life complicated? Is it too much space to keep up with, too many possessions crowded into your space, too many entangled emotions and relational messes in your life? What ruins your day for you? How do we gain perspective on such issues so they do not consume our energy and attention? Are you able to find joy in each day you live? Are you discovering your Wisdom Years? The heaviness of past battles, leftover hurts, disappointments, unreleased sorrow can keep our interior lives from experiencing the lightness of being that turns the rest of life into a dance rather than a war zone.

Personally, I find this particular life project to be quite demanding: to keep my attitude positive, my awareness tuned into living well, my body in the best health possible, my spiritual life active and nurtured. The calling to live well simply cannot be taken for granted. It takes stamina, courage, and tenacity to live with wisdom and joy. One day, when Cleve and I were walking along the trail in the blazing sun, I was hot and tired, beginning to wonder why we were doing this. In other words, my cranky was about to explode! I caught myself in this irrational mood, stopped dead still on the trail, and gave birth to a brand-new idea. The key to lighten my heart, unclutter my head, and set free my soul is one thing: *adaptability*! (Do you remember Billy Crystal in *City Slickers* searching for the "one thing" to change his attitude from dour and depressed to happy and loving again?)

Beginning in our fifties, aging requires that we become more adaptable in so many ways that we can feel overwhelmed if we don't pay attention to this reality. I have several close friends who currently sense the first nudges of this truth: The body starts to break down at this age for sure, beginning with small, annoying aches that soon increase to acute pain when the aging process becomes full blown! First, of course, is the way our bodies function. It takes more hours of sleep, better food, and ample exercise simply to keep the older body in some semblance of working order. We are no longer running new vehicles! The minute I cheat or cut back on the basics—food, sleep and exercise—to keep myself going, I begin to pay a price. My youth is waning, and I can no longer abuse my body the way I did in my previous years of life, with a stressful lifestyle and other unhealthy habits. So I must adapt.

Second, I find that as I age I need to know more about my body. When I was young, I did not pay attention to what made it run well. I just used my body, and it did what I wanted it to do. But now as seniors, it's a different game, isn't it? So now I ask myself: *What must I relinquish that I used to love to do that simply no longer works for me?* Jogging was the first activity to go, recommended by my doctor who was trying to help me save my knees. (Thanks, Steve!) Now I walk and hike. Downhill skiing had to go—now I snowshoe. Backpacking was the next to go—now I car camp. I had to sell my canoe. Now, I occasionally go on a cruise. Mountain biking was no longer easy or fun—now I have a bike designed for seniors called a "townie."

Late nights and early mornings shifted—now I need eight hours of sleep. My difficult yoga class no longer worked for me, and now I do less strenuous yoga in the comfort of my home. A diet that included beef and pork ceased. Now, I eat mostly vegetarian with some fish and chicken occasionally. Caffeine drinks started to bother my heart—now it's only decaf for me! Alcoholic drinks vanished from my diet—now it's the occasional glass of Reisling or Sangria for me.

Without a doubt, many seniors continue extreme activities late into their nineties, so my list is not the norm for everyone reading this book. It's simply *my* list. As an example one ninety-six-year-old friend here in Santa Fe only recently halted his downhill skiing adventures while I had to surrender skiing years ago. However, in the meantime, Marv has had to relinquish other activities.

Others I know have had to surrender quite different activities they love. Recently, while lunching with a new friend, we were sharing our "aging" woes over the things we must surrender due to age. He said, "I just realized recently that I have to give up playing the bells at my church." Noticing how sad he seemed about this revelation, I offered him my "adaptability" plan. "Why don't you take up some other form of music, even if all you can do is listen and learn? What's on your music bucket list? Why not give yourself a new experience with music?" His eyes sparked with hope. I will check back with him in a few months and see how he is doing.

As we age each of us has to let go of activities we have enjoyed throughout our younger years. Why don't you make your own list?

What have you had to surrender due to age and aching muscles, and what have you put in its place? I have had to adapt over and over again to my aging body. You will also.

So here's the deal. We could become resentful and frustrated at of all of this letting go of our beloved habits, activities and rituals, or we can adapt to these changes in our lives. At first, I did what most Baby Boomers do. I pushed too hard for too long until I nearly killed myself with stress and stretching my body way past what it was willing to withstand on my behalf. I became depressed as I watched my favorite outdoor sports get the best of me. I stopped participating in an active life for several years, turning all my attention to my career, all the while resenting the whole process. Then, of course, I gained weight and became even more discontented. I began to feel that I could not live the quality of life I desired. Rather than adapting to my new reality, I just gave up and mostly pouted about it, even growing somewhat depressed. Retirees become complainers and cranks with this attitude, and I was in danger of joining those ranks.

After I read Fr. Rohr's book, I realized that I should address this issue or my senior years would not be fruitful and enjoyable. So I designed the pilgrimages, the first one testing my physical strength and courage. I adapted over and over again on that journey with Cleve. And by the time I returned to Santa Fe, I understood how to relate more adequately to my body—by adapting to the activities I *could* do and relinquishing those I should no longer do.

The key to success in this new understanding of my physical limitations is my inner attitude. Rather than resenting the loss of several of my favorite activities, I have instead found new ways to stay active and involved in the game of life utilizing the body of a seventy-year-old. This, in turn, has completely revolutionized my mental and emotional life. Seeking meaning and purpose in my newly discovered lifestyle merged into a love for walking and a fresh outlook on aging. A *mantra* fills my head when I come up against a limitation of my physical skills—*adapt, adapt, adapt—stay in the game, but adapt.*

Adapting to what life offers us has its home in an interior quest for courage and strength. I stated earlier that aging takes courage.

Anyone over seventy knows this for sure, and there may be younger seniors who have also begun to discover this too often obscure truth. As the body and mind begin to play tricks on us, resisting our desire to remain young and active, we need enormous stamina to stay centered and focused on living intentionally with the body we actually inhabit. The heart follows suit if the mind gives in to unhappiness, apathy, rage or even stoicism. Our emotions become limited and stilted when we surrender to the demon of the fear of growing old or losing our daily life as we once knew it. A family friend calls this "becoming anesthetized."

Facing that mesa wall that Cleve expected me to climb took a kind of courage I have seldom had to face, physical *courage*. As a child I climbed easily and skillfully to the tops of buildings, football field viewing towers, rooftops, trees, even the highest diving board at our local community pool. No problem or fears. But somehow as I became an adult my climbing comfort zone became compromised, and I developed a fear of heights. I remember in my late sixties, I climbed a set of stairs in the Tybee Island lighthouse in Georgia with my youngest daughter, holding my breath most of the way, wondering when I would faint. But these stairs were indoors, with rails and concrete steps. Even this frightening climb did not demand of me what crawling up that mesa wall did with no edges, toeholds or walls to catch me. But something took hold of me, determination perhaps. "I came here to test myself, and I will at least give this a try!"

Every step was excruciating, laced through and through with fear. Every inch of progress required intense concentration. Every breath hurt my lungs and chest. My heart was pounding so loudly I could hear it beating. The jagged rock edges scratched my hands and shins. I bled and climbed on. A memory crowded itself into my mind as I moved one leg and then the other slowly up the crevice of the wall.

Just weeks before her death, her frail form lying on the bed, her eyes bright with tears, she stared into mine and asked, "Will I have the courage to face my death? I don't want to be afraid in front of my children." I was hardly prepared for Pam's question and do not believe I did a particularly good job of reassuring her. As her pastor and confidante through this dying process, I knew I was supposed to say the right thing at this moment, but I felt her raging fright in my very bones. I grabbed her hand, stroked her arm, and waited for the fear to pass from both of us. Finally, I spoke quietly, "Pam, your children trust you. Whatever you do, they will believe in you to the very end." Giving me a weak smile, she closed her eyes to rest.

Trust. After this memory flashed through my mind, I realized that I had to trust myself to get the job done, just as Pam had to do to attend her dying. The lesson I gained from her dying words is that we are still absorbing life lessons even until our final breath. In her case, Pam had to trust herself enough to muster the courage to face relinquishing her children and husband as she left this earth. In my case, hanging onto that mesa wall like a lizard—nothing as dramatic as Pam's story—made me acutely aware that this climb framed a living metaphor for my own death. If I did not find the courage I needed in this moment of life, and trust myself to find my inner self-determination to keep climbing, then how would I face my own aging process and eventual death? Aging demands that we turn our interior lives inside out in order to handle what is ahead, which is mostly vulnerability and loss.

While I don't ask each of you to go to the desert and climb a mesa wall to discover your own courage and learn how to trust yourself, I do encourage you to find *something* that replicates this mission inside your own interior story. What do you need or want to do that will provide you with the vision and commitment to nurture within your own soul the stamina and courage it takes to age and die? For most of us such issues have never come up before. Facing such questions is unexpected and often unwelcome. Each day in the life of most seniors is a challenge of some sort. The exterior and interior work of intentional aging is relentless and intense. So we might as well take on the project with gusto and bring ourselves into the process with awareness—mindfulness, some might say.

I ask you to seriously consider these questions: What is your plan to manifest the understanding needed to know yourself as a senior adult? Where is your courage grounded so that you will know where to go for strength when needed? Do you trust yourself enough to take on the difficult quest of opening the door into the Wisdom Years? Are you willing to risk the journey into your soul to learn about yourself in ways that may surprise or even disappoint you? Can you face the truth of who you really are?

There is one concluding lesson I wish to share with you from my first pilgrimage. In his book *Why Time Flies*, Alan Burdick writes, "Much of what we do in the present is done reflexively, habit is the enemy of mindful thought. Why don't we think more about the present when we are in it?" These words strike me as insightful: Why *don't* we live in the present when we are in it? I suspect the answer has something to do with becoming mindful of our lives.

Living in the open, out of doors, in the elements of wind, rain, sun, cold, and dark in the Arizona desert began to create for me a new rhythm of time. When I am in my Santa Fe world, I find that I am normally guided by a clock and the structures of suburban life. Meals, meetings, chores, putting out the trash barrels, calls from our children, daily news programs, hair appointments, trips to Albuquerque. All of these events form a tapestry of time within which I live, usually without much tension. In retirement, I wake up fairly close to the same time each day; eat when the news is on, and do the tasks, errands and work that the day ahead has scheduled. Daily life when released from employment does feel as if I am in charge and free to do as I wish. But this belief can be quite inaccurate. Habits do form, even in retirement, that relate to clock time, usually without our being very aware of this daily occurrence. Beginning early after I left my career, I found myself living by the clock just as I had during my institutional life.

Before my pilgrimages I had begun to long for time without measurement, days without patterns, deliberately broken habits but felt convinced I would never know this experience. I even began to wonder if it is possible to live without reference to clock time. I learned on this first pilgrimage that I could live more naturally in relation to time.

With no television to watch and phones that did not operate in the desert, Cleve and I kept pretty much to a "what do you want to do next?" mode. I seldom remembered what day of the week it was, nor did I have access to the exact time of day. I allowed my stomach to tell me when to eat and my fatigue to inform me that I needed sleep. I crawled into my tent every evening after the sky darkened and did not emerge until the sun hit the walls of the tent again to warm it. In my nylon house, time had no measurement such that the tyranny of clock time actually faded.

As Cleve and I hiked the trails, I noticed that time flattened and stretched. One segment of the day seemed elongated, another passed by in a flash. On this pilgrimage I began to pay close attention to my orientation to time—because, aging is precisely about time, mostly running out of it! I slowly awakened to learn to live in the moment. (What we are involved in at the moment is all that is truly authentic.) I felt my body begin to fully relax, maybe for the first time in years. I became mindful of all that surrounded me. I was aware of the feel of the wind on my skin, the sun beating down on my bare arms, the sweat on my face under the brim of my hat. My eyes could see distances as I developed a renewed interest in horizons. My ears perked up at the sounds of desert birds. "I am still alive!" I thought.

John Donohue described it best when he wrote in his book *Anam Cara*, "When time is reduced to linear progress, it is emptied of presence." His words spoke to me as if I were hearing them for the very first time. Yes! This is it! Presence...time in this moment reveals Presence. These thoughts would come back to haunt me on my fourth pilgrimage.

In our urban world, everything we experience is close up these days, mostly screens. We can seldom see a horizon. I believe this is why the institutional world manages to keep its inhabitants addicted to the idea that shopping and work are so much more important and exciting than they really are. I also believe this is why today's children are so out of touch with nature and themselves. They are constantly contained in buildings, or classrooms, or houses, or cars, or on city streets, in strollers, or even locked into fenced yards. Children seldom see a horizon. Being out of doors, either in deserts or on mountaintops, allows us to appreciate horizons, edges of the earth that lure us into adventure. Our perspective about the ultimate meaning of life becomes more accurate and authentic.

Seeking new horizons as seniors can easily become of less and less interest as we unwittingly allow our daily worlds to grow smaller and smaller, closing in on us. We tend to do this because it is easier, less complicated, more comfortable not to challenge ourselves. This tendency is the death knell of the Wisdom Years. Paying attention to the cycles of time in our lives gives us access to a resource for living fully, with energy and excitement. When was the last time you were truly excited about something? When have you considered the possibilities for accomplishment, learning, expanding as a retiree? Seniors, I have noticed, often lose their excitement for surprise and spontaneity that comes so naturally to our grandchildren. To repeat myself, I suspect this is why grandparents and grandchildren get along so well—the young ones teach the older ones about how time should really be lived, with imagination, play, spontaneity, joy. Time becomes heavy for seniors as it speeds along toward our demise, unless we break the spell and live in the present with sheer delight.

A neighbor said to me recently, "Why don't you stay home more? You travel and go too much." He did not approve of my pilgrimages, especially the three that I took without my spouse, which, for a Texan dominant male-type, was an idea he could not handle. I responded passionately to his query, "I am not ready for the grave! Life still excites me. I have many places to go, much to see and do. I am not done with the adventure of my life. It's not time for the sofa or nursing home yet!"

You might imagine his face with this response.

CHAPTER 4:
HOME IS NOT A PLACE
PILGRIMAGE NO. 2: EXTERIOR STORY

To seek to be alone is a radical act.
—David Whyte

One of the joys of aging is that you have more time to be still.
—John O'Donohue

Standing with my duffel baggage in front of the airport hotel in Manchester, England, I find myself feeling like a middle-school student again—that uncomfortable feeling that so many of us remember on the first day of classes in a new school at a new grade level. Mortified, really. Restlessly insecure and unsure of how to even start this new pilgrimage, I paste a grimace on my face at the situation in which I find myself. At age sixty-nine, I would think feelings like these would be long past. But here I am, wondering what in the world I have done to myself by signing up for a poetry/walking tour with the Irish English poet David Whyte and thirty complete strangers. I invited no one to go with me on this trip and am now regretting that decision! Though I have long reveled in David's writings, to travel so many miles just to spend a few hours in the middle of nowhere with this mysterious poet suddenly seems quite foolish.

In the midst of my embarrassed reverie, a striking man with twinkling blue eyes walks up to me only to query with a shy grin, "Are you here waiting for the David Whyte tour?" As I nod my awkward affirmation, he continues his comments, "Looks like we are the two introverts in the group." I glance around the open-air public space. Everyone else is gathered in clumps of threes and fours, chatting vivaciously, smiling, laughing, in some cases even hugging.

"I guess we are." I chuckle nervously, expelling a sigh of inward relief that someone has acknowledged that I am in the right place at the right time.

The vans pull up that will haul all of us to "the farm," where we will live in remote retreat for a week together. Our gathered menagerie piles into the vehicles, helter-skelter, no order at all. Great! Just my favorite thing in the world: to be jammed together in small spaces with total strangers for a long ride to God only knows where. Why in the world did I think this was a good idea? I know myself, this self who does not like to be an introvert in uncomfortable extrovert settings. At this point I begin to berate myself. After a professional life in which I spent days upon years as a public speaker, teacher, preacher, administrator, mentor, and advisor, how in the world am I not yet adjusted to this sort of gathering? But I am not. At least for the moment I have enough presence of mind to be aware of my discomfort and vow to work on it—again!

Then I remember the lesson from my pilgrimage to Chaco Canyon—adapt! I make an internal reminder to myself: "Take mindfulness training when I return home!" (Little did I know at this point that following my final pilgrimage of the year, I would indeed sit in a life changing mindfulness workshop with spiritual teacher John Bruna that would bring awareness and peace to my psyche.) The life lessons in this second pilgrimage begin early as I acknowledge the courage it has taken for me to place myself in a situation where I am apprehensive. "Good! I am on track to stretch and grow once again—one of the benefits of the pilgrimages as I designed them," I remind myself.

Our temptation as we age is to halt our own growth and forfeit the uncomfortable. Why should we, after all, step out of our comfort zone? Isn't life ours to control and decide at this point in time, after all those years of being held accountable by and to others? Yet I am keenly aware that this pushing of my personal boundaries will lead to growth for me as I move boldly toward my Wisdom Years. All of us have patterns and predilections. These usually intensify as we age. That jolly soul named Bill who was a dear friend for years only became warmer and more welcoming as he aged, even until he died with dementia. That cranky neighbor who invariably complained about everything when he was younger, has only become grouchier as he ages. To become comfortable, challenging our lifelong behaviors exposes another crucial aging task just at a time when we want to stay "just like we are," expecting others to adapt to us. Eradicating our self-constructed boundaries as we age is even more essential as we advance toward our senior years with grace and grit. Try it! This is *not* easy!

Despite the usual daily drizzle (it is England, after all!) an idyllic scene opens to all of us as we arrive at our retreat site. A rustic white fifteenth century farmhouse materializes as the vans round the corner of a long, winding drive. Even in the grayness of the day, the house seems inviting and cozy as it hunkers down in the thick dampness of the farmland. Black and white cows graze lazily across richly verdant pastures, while clucking chickens busily search for food in their wire pen. This picturesque moment resides perfectly sketched into the landscape overlooking pristine Conistan Lake. My overactive brain begins to calm down in this pastoral setting as I realize things will be okay.

The retreat participants are assigned to various rooms scattered among several buildings. I end up with a tall, lanky, red-haired young surgeon as my roommate for the week we will spend together in one of the remodeled cottages. Though we have nothing much in common in our external lives (our ages and life interests are too far apart), we are comfortably compatible. She will do just fine for the week, I muse. A couple of hours pass as we settle into our space; she takes the bed closest to the window as I settle into the space by the closet door. We are both quiet as we unpack our gear.

Soon all of us are summoned to a sumptuous dinner over in the main house. As my colleagues and I fill our stomachs with the chef's best work and good wines warm our bodies, gentle conversation begins to blossom among the various table groupings. We haphazardly begin to sort out the social arrangements for the week. The dinner hour comes to an end, and I scoot off to my cottage space, not interested in the evening bar life of the younger members. My introvert self at this point is still gasping for air. One of my favorite descriptions of myself comes to mind, "I am peopled out," I mutter, after this day of intense proximity to the rest of the group.

"To seek to be alone is a radical act." David Whyte utters these words to us the next morning as we begin our first session with him. "Is he reading my mind?" I wonder. Looking around the snug upstairs living room of the farmhouse where we gather each morning for our sessions with David, I secretly study all of the faces in the room, faces of people I do not yet know. I am quite aware that I will not stay in touch with these people once the retreat is over. I have not come on this retreat to create a new set of friends. I have come for my own purpose and growth. This is my second pilgrimage designed to reawaken my poetic muse and to experience the enlivening of my soul after so many years in the academic and church worlds, where my psyche began to slumber from the tedious daily grind. Thus, David's words split asunder my heart and mind. I *am* seeking to be alone, even in the midst of this energetic group of people. I am here to soak up the poetry, music, landscape—to reawaken my soul to its deepest longings and to the sacred space of my upcoming Wisdom Years.

To desire to be alone in today's hectic and hyper-connected world (not to be confused with being isolated or lonely, which is an entirely different issue) is perhaps a bizarre quest for most of us. David's statement concerning the radical act of choosing to be alone is quite startling given modern cultures. The planet itself surges like a beehive of activity with lights that never go off, available electronic connections 24-7, people merging and moving nonstop. Most seniors can recite a litany of how busy their children and grandchildren are these days, and many of us have been swept up into the vortex of those lives. People seem to move in herds, afraid of alone time, the time necessary to develop an inner life and intimacy with self.

Seniors often face a dual dilemma: First is the sad reality of isolation due to health issues or other lifestyle complications like the loss of a mate or having to move away from family or friends. Such isolation or loneliness makes it difficult to desire being alone as a spiritual or emotional discipline. Many seniors suffer in silence from a forced isolation that in the end often causes their death. Yet to seek to be alone in order to contemplate our life journey is spiritually and psychologically an essential act of nurturing self-knowledge. To find balance in being alone without being lonely creates a vital pathway guiding us into our Wisdom Years.

The second dilemma that can trap us is a modern problem, to be overly busy and caught up with too much to do. This situation can be caused by too much "yes" in our lives—agreeing to an overwhelming number of obligations and promises such that our days are too full. Seniors are experts at doing this to themselves, I have detected. I've had more than one person say to me, "I thought retirement would give me time for my own pursuits. But I never have any time!"

As I sit on the cushioned window seat among my retreat colleagues who are scattered around the room, enraptured by the poet as I am, my introvert self moves from frustration that I earlier felt isolated (self-imposed, of course), to a realization that I am deliberately choosing my aloneness in the midst of the group. I am on a mission. I am not intending to be unfriendly, for sure. I join in for all shared meals, sitting with various people to learn who they are and why they chose to attend the retreat. During the van rides to various hiking sites, I chatter with others about their life and family stories. My favorites were a couple of Irish sisters on the trip who signed up to do an homage to their mother who had recently passed away. I loved their quiet, gentle presences! On the trails I find hiking buddies each day, all with interesting stories to share. It is not my intention to be rude on this pilgrimage, only to be true to my task of self-discernment and growth.

During the unscheduled times I escape to my cottage for journaling, meditation, poetry writing, and reflection. And I make no apology for these behaviors, as I realize I am deliberately choosing to be alone for an intended purpose. As soon as I have made this connection for myself, the entire experience of the retreat changes from one of feeling isolated and lonely (the introvert's prison cell) to one of ease and acceptance. I am on this retreat to begin to write a new story for myself. I have chosen to be alone on this particular pilgrimage in order to learn the lesson of the *radical act of being alone* after so many years of being with others in my professional world, in my institutional life. It is time to become reacquainted with myself and begin to sort out who I am as a soon-to-be septuagenarian.

There is such a temptation as we move from our institutional years to our intentional years to recreate the same lives we had when we were engaged in our careers. We surround ourselves with activities and people to look busy and keep ourselves in the game of life. But the Wisdom Years call for an entirely different set of commitments and insights. To possess quality of life during our senior years requires the ability to be radically alone from time to time and to feel content with this change in our days. To do this, we have to appreciate who we are enough to be comfortable in our own skin. Quite a challenge for many!

The days in the poetry/walking retreat begin to have a placid rhythm to them. We sit in session with David and his musicians in the mornings and hike in the afternoons, with free time set aside for socializing in the evening hours. Every day there is a takeaway from the presentation, some wisp of wisdom that David gifts to us in his quiet, thoughtful way. Soothed by the music of his voice and the mystical tone of his speech, I slowly begin to return to my whole self as I let his words sink into my heart and mind. Sitting day after day in the presence of this poet delights my senses and awakens my dream world. Poetry begins to flow again inside my soul. There is an odd way in which writing poetry isolates me. To write a poem is definitely a solitary exercise of vulnerability spilling onto the page. At another level of my being, however, poetry manifests the most intimate use of language possible, and this intimacy creates the passionate life for me. I am now grateful I screwed up my courage to attend this retreat.

Our afternoons are spent walking the trails of the English Lake District, straight up into the mists of the mountaintops, spiraling down into the lush valleys laced with streams. Purple foxglove form clumps around the paths, just waiting to be touched. (I learned the hard way that I should not do this since I am allergic to the plant!) Such an exquisite landscape I have not before seen. The earth matches the poetry we receive each day: deep, dark, damp, luring us higher and higher until we are out of breath and longing for respite. David scampers up the mountainsides like a frisky goat, while his students struggle to climb the rugged edges before us. Some of us, including me, fall behind from time to time. I must confess, this hiking is nothing like the Superstition Mountains, where sure-footed plodding on switchback trails will get you somewhere eventually. To climb straight up in the Lake District requires skill on the narrow and slippery granite paths. I soon realize I have met my match in these mountains. My age is surely my limitation. I am facing my waterloo on this pilgrimage! I never expected this to happen!

On one particular hike, I begin to reminisce about my first pilgrimage and the toughness of those hikes. I felt so good each day as Cleve and I accomplished our chosen hike. The climb up the mesa wall had been exhilarating and had rejuvenated me. I thought, *My almost seventy-year-old body* will *work for me!* But here on this slick, wet, and vertically rigorous trail to the top of an English mountain, I realize my first pilgrimage has given me a false sense of bravado. As I watch younger members of the group scamper up the trails, and the older ones (my group) slog along, clutching at grass clumps for balance, slipping and sliding on the stony trail, I know the number of years I have lived is real. Here is my Mt. Everest, and I am becoming quite aware that I will not succeed to the summit. The heavy sense of sure defeat begins to invade my mind as I, along with several others my age, turn around and begin to climb back down, clinging to the face of the mountain so we do not fall.

Half of this eclectic poetry group includes people over fifty, most of whom lurch and lunge up the mountain trails each day, out of breath and groaning. Some stumble. Some actually fall. Some rebel at the climb and refuse to go any farther. Others scramble up the wet peaks with David, the hearty few who are young and brave. These folks have the bragging rights every night at dinner for making it to the misty mountaintops. We are a motley crew, each wrestling with our own skills and intentions on these hikes. This is our pattern for the week together. The group divides rapidly into two groups: those who came to struggle and grow, and those who came to play.

One thrilling hike for me does not go high but goes long. David's crew ferries us on a boat ride on one of the lakes in the area, dumps us on shore, and leaves us to walk the seven miles back to the vans. Having done more than seven miles on several of my hikes with Cleve, this particular day is easy for me. I am in great shape for this! I revel in the bright sunny day, the pace of the hilly somewhat straight trail that allows me to view the landscape rather than watch where I am planting my feet. For some of the group, this lengthy trail creates a challenge for which they are unprepared, but one without options. The only way back to the vans is to walk. So walk we do!

At one point on this trail, our hikers come face to face with another large group, schoolgirls, all with flowers in their hair. As they walk merrily along the pathways, the students sing or call out to each other with high-pitched giggles. Finally, I can no longer stand the suspense. What in the world are they doing out here on a school day, decked out with flowers in their hair? So I stop a clump of them and pointedly ask, "Why do you have flowers in your hair on a hiking trail?" They laugh at my question, but easily begin to interrupt each other trying to tell me the story. This is their last day of school. Excitement for the freedom of the summer months is palpable. Their joviality reminds me of my excitement each year as a child, when school released us from its tentacles and allowed us to escape into sandals, swimming pools, backyard barbecues and nighttime games of hide-and-seek. As the girls worm their way past us on the slender trail, I ponder, "Why, as we age, do our memories of childhood come closer and closer, while our adult institutional years begin to fade?"

After listening to his poetry and watching his love affair with the land beneath his feet, I realize David Whyte is a "nature mystic." Since I have long labeled myself as the same sort of human being, I easily fall into the intention of the retreat: to bond us to poetry and nature, to help us recover ourselves from the lost places within.

The gift of this pilgrimage for me becomes a renewal of my primal bond with nature, an attachment I have held since my childhood. Having recently escaped the institutional world, I am quite aware of the almost sinister plot it held to destroy my soul. The institutional world locks us indoors, enslaving us to our computers or classrooms, office cubicles or factory lines. Retirement has provided for me the source of my grounding in the natural world: clouds and creatures, fields and forests, winds and wildness simply because I can walk out of doors at any moment I desire.

The lesson here is a staunch reminder of our creation as human beings: To shift from institutional life to the intentional life invites us to connect or reconnect with our natural created selves. For some, this might be gardening, like my friend in Pecos, New Mexico, who delightedly plants her vegetable garden every spring. For others a connection with nature is through sports, like my neighbor who plays golf almost every day. For others, this connection might occur when driving cross-country, making stops at all of the National Parks. Still for many, the link to nature comes from the simple act of walking their dog twice a day. The path I have chosen allows me to be *in* and *with* nature by walking every day that I am physically able.

Aging is, if nothing else, the process of returning to the origins of our birth, dust to dust, a natural phenomenon. Some of the unhappiest people I see in my public or in my personal worlds are those who are completely out of touch with nature. There seems to be for them no reason to seek an encounter with the natural world. Thus they fail to realize that as human beings made of water and stardust (according to astrophysicist Neil deGrasse Tyson) we, too, belong to nature. These folks take the artificial world entirely too seriously. In turn, angst, anger and depression appear all too frequently, which is deadly to our quality, and even the quantity, of life. In order to accept our dying, we must identify with and accept the processes of nature. What better way to do this than discover a way to connect with the natural world?

Even if all you are able to do is put up a hummingbird feeder to watch the daily dance of this delightful tiny bird, do this! If all you can do is walk around the block with its brick and mortar buildings and sidewalks, the sun and the wind are still out there. Find an excuse to get outside if at all possible. Scientists have recognized the relationship of nature to health to the extent that our local community college in Santa Fe has created a program of study focused on ecology and health. The travesty of aging is that many are forced inside, never able to breathe in the fresh air. This will kill us quickly, folks. Unless you are on your deathbed, find a way to get outside every day! Take a deep breath. Feel the sun, or rain, or wind, or moon on your skin and face. Smell the air. Stare at the stars and moon every evening possible. Become aware of the natural world around you and join it. This mindful awareness is, frankly, the key to a high-quality life!

The lesson of simplicity rises once again in this pilgrimage, just as it did in the first one. In one of his presentations, David solemnly stares at us, pausing for a long, breathless moment and then says, "What you need is much less than you have." And then he pauses again to allow his words to sink into our minds and hearts.

Here again is the directive to downsize, go smaller, leaner, simpler. For myself, I took this admonition to mean that retirement is a discipline of letting go of as much of our life baggage and possessions as is possible. Our penchant in America for buying stuff is an addiction that only rears its ugly head when you have to move it all to another place. Then we come to understand how much unnecessary "stuff," (to use George Carlin's potent word) we own. This is why storage units abound in America! If we pay attention, retirement provides a blessed awakening about the joy of going simple and allows us to give away, donate, share, sell.

In this Wednesday morning session with our talented poet, I internally acknowledge that in my Santa Fe world, I am struggling mightily with letting go of a closet full of professional clothing. The frugal lessons of my childhood make it difficult for me to relinquish clothes that are not worn out, even though I do not imagine ever using them again. So every few months I meander into that closet, pull out a few things, take them to the donation store, and feel good again—for a few weeks. Then, the business suits and clerical robes stare at me once more, creating guilt for keeping them and more guilt for wishing they would disappear into whatever vortex clothes can vanish when we are done with them. I make a pledge right then and there: I *will* banish these useless clothes from my closet when I return home. *What I have is definitely much more than what I need.*

And the "elephant in the room" here is all the baggage from my interior life that needs a swift spring cleaning, for sure. In this case I definitely have more entanglements than necessary that must be released for me to step across the threshold into my Wisdom Years. However, I will peruse that topic in the next chapter, when I explore the interior work I take home with me from this particular pilgrimage.

On an unusually balmy day, our tour crew hauls us quite a distance to a trail close to Dove Cottage, the home of William Wordsworth in the village of Grasmere. Across the busy street from the main shops, a walking path winds its way up the mountainside. This walk appeals to most of us as we spill out of the vans in anticipation of our venture. However, before long, all the hikers have once again split into two groups, those who can briskly assault the mountain with David and those who need a slower pace. I place myself in the second group. At first the trail, while daunting, does not seem impossible. Trekking up the steep path, our little group of faithful hikers is strung out like a snake, huffing and puffing as we pull ourselves forward. I do not dare to look for the pinnacle of this challenge, fearing I would give up the hike. I really want to complete this one and get to the crest of the mountain, not only for the view but also for my own sense of accomplishment.

Soon the slower group needs to rest. We stop on a high, stony prominence overlooking stunning views of the river valley below. Three of us drop our daypacks and find medium-sized boulders on which to perch in order to take long, greedy slugs of water from our bottles. My legs already ache. Randomly some of us fall into a conversation about Baby Boomer memories: the sixties and all its chaos and madness, and the crazy politics of the Vietnam War. For some reason I never fail to be surprised at how wistfully Boomers rattle off the names of their favorite musicians and bands from that long-gone era, and I'm no different. Creedance Clearwater Revival comes to my mind as I start to hum a verse from one of their songs under my breath. Then I find myself toe-tapping to *I Heard It Through the Grapevine,* remembering that I had danced wildly and madly to this song in my younger years. Such good memories...Baby Boomer music is the best!

The conversation intensifies as three of us descend into a zany discussion about contemporary life and politics. This conversation determines our fate for the day. Without our noticing, the rest of the group has pulled out and moved on up the mountainside. I look up and see our compatriots crawling like ants on the ledges high above us. Chagrined, my two partners and I realize we will not be able to catch up with the group. We resolve to head back down the mountain to the agreed upon meeting place and simply wait there until the group returns. This is our first mistake.

The second is taking a wrong turn down the mountain, soon to become lost in the maze of trails that crisscross our paths. We are lost only in the sense that we are on the wrong trail. We realize that we must go *down* the mountain because the village lies below us. But we do not know how to correct our mistake and return to our designated trail. In a quandary, we stand by a tall wooden gate to collaborate, but to no avail. None of us recognizes where we are or how to locate the trail. After a solid half hour passes, a slender brown-haired male about thirty years of age walks up to us and quickly guesses our dilemma. "Are you lost?" he asks with a heavy accent.

With embarrassment, I mumble quietly, "Yes, we are." The young man grins at us and laughs, "I am your guide sent to take you down the mountain." And so he does. The journey down is not without a fascinating conversation about the "Brexit" vote that has just recently occurred. I discern that his accent is not British, so I ask him what the vote means to him personally. Since our guide resides in England through a work permit, he shares his distress that he will, as an alien, lose his job and be forced to return to his own country, where there is no work. Fear is evident on his face and in the tremor in his voice. As he guides us to our location, we wave an awkward goodbye to him, for none of us knows how to offer him comfort.

While we are waiting for the vans to arrive, the two men with me take off to search for warm cups of coffee in a shop nearby. By this time, late afternoon, the day has begun to turn damp and cold again, surrendering the sun to thick, billowy clouds above. Feeling the chill in the air, I sit down on a wooden bench beside the now empty main street, pull my jacket tighter on my body, zip up the front, hunch over my shoulders against the wind and begin ruminating on the concept of "home."

After our orphan guide's tale, I wonder where he considers home, England or Poland? Or is he lost in some strange space between the two? Over the years of my life, home has had several emanations. In my younger years, home meant house, parents and siblings, friends, school. In my adult years before these senior years, home has been marriage, children, mortgage, repairs, entertaining, even sanctuary. But as I cross over into my seventieth year of life, home is a concept that has become nebulous to me—not a place, not a time, not even a group of people.

Sucking in my breath against the growing cold of the waning day, I begin to mentally rummage through my list of retired friends and family. How do they consider the idea of home? Many of my friends have stayed close to their children and grandchildren, remaining in the same towns and cities where they spent their institutional years. Life resembles that of their institutional lives, continuing along the familiar paths of the previous years of their lives with many of the same friends, same grocery store, same church or club, same activities. I wonder how these seniors will define home for themselves as they age. What will be the core of this idea for them?

In the meantime other seniors move away from the communities where they reared children and lived as employees. In many cases, they have left behind close friends, children, grandchildren and extended family simply for the adventure of living in another setting. Some have entered into retirement communities in Arizona or Florida, Colorado or California.

One set of friends moved to Mexico. I find myself wondering what they felt they needed to escape. Another couple from California simply sold their home, picked up and moved to Santa Fe without having even seen the town, because they wanted to retire to an entirely different place and space with a better economic factor. Faculty friends of mine shifted homes from the middle of the country to the East and West coasts, to nestle among trees and lakes. Some seniors I know have the luxury of owning two homes, one for wintering and another for the summer months. They move back and forth all year, living nomadic lives in a sense. Still other Baby Boomers are participating in the burgeoning phenomenon called "senior trailer parks" springing up around America's landscapes. Such homes are for those seniors who enjoy life on the run. These places fill faster than they can be built.

Home, at least for Baby Boomers, is a moving target. To retire is to live where we want to be, not where our former jobs are and where our families live. Thomas Friedman in his book, *Thank You for Being Late* writes, "With so much changing so fast, it's easier than ever today for people to feel a loss of 'home' in the deepest sense."

Thus, I raise this question: What is home to a person moving into the Wisdom Years? It seems obvious that the familiar definition of family and lodging no longer applies to seniors given the statistics about senior mobility. Facing the reality that just as we long to "settle down" and "never move again" (as some seniors are known for saying), our reality is such that we are likely to move several times in these years before we die. These shifts in location will form a rather predictable pattern: from the home of our institutional years to a down-sized house, or perhaps a retirement village, from there to an independent living apartment or residence with an adult child, to assisted living, to a nursing home, to hospice, to the grave. Most of us have many moves remaining, given the aging process in our culture. Thus, as nascent elderlies should we not attend to the question, "Where is home for us?"

With the aging experience in motion, we would be unwise to locate our sense of home in a given structure or even in relationships with family members or friendships. And this is not an easy thought to have or sentence to write because we are so very oriented toward our sense of place and our relationships. As we age, our relationships become even more necessary. But if we are honest with ourselves and with each other, we come to realize in the Wisdom Years that even our relationships are transient. No. Home cannot be located in a structure or a relationship as we age. Home has to become an *interior space* where we reside regardless of where our bodies are located or to whom we are emotionally attached.

The *interior life* unveils itself as "home base" if we are to adapt to the reality of aging as it unfolds. And this interior life requires tender nurturing and care, as if it is our prized garden. Home can no longer be a fixed space or place during the Wisdom Years—our authentic home calls for an orientation toward life itself from within.

Fr. Rohr states this idea most clearly:

> The whole story is set in the matrix of seeking to find home and then to return there, and thus refining and defining what home really is. Home is both the beginning and the end. Home is not a sentimental concept at all, but an inner compass and a North Star at the same time. It is a metaphor for the soul.

There are no truer words than these.

Suddenly I pop back from my reveries into my current situation as a white van pulls up beside me. I gather my belongings from the bench while a thought resonates through my body, *This is precisely what I am doing on this pilgrimage with David Whyte and his troubadours. I am relocating my "interior home."*

On our final day of this transformative poetry/hiking retreat, our eclectic group is loaded up once more into the roomy vans to be driven to Castlerigg Stone Circle near Keswick. As we arrive, a mist falls on us from the dark, heavy clouds above. Imposing stones circling a large patch of green grass spread out in front of me. Having previously seen stone circles in Ireland, I know what I am about to witness will be sheer magic, but I have yet no idea of the majesty and mystery of this particular site. Velvety green mountains surround the stone circle, creating another circle. The sky looms ominously over us, promising to drench us at any moment. My feet somehow feel light above the earth, as if I am hardly touching the ground.

As I turn my head from side to side to view the variously shaped stones, a haunting sound arises from beside one of the stately megaliths. Searching for the origin of the sound, I hear two of our musicians softly singing *Abide with Me* in a cappella tones, one of them gently strumming an Irish drum. This piece of music pulls me back into the roots of my Baptist childhood, and tears start to roll down my face. How beautiful are these poignant chords begging for the comfort and presence of the Divine in the midst of this Neolithic sacred site. Don't we all need *something* to abide with us as we move closer and closer to our demise? I vow on the spot that this hymn will become part of my memorial ritual upon my death.

Even here in this sacred space, I become aware of details and tasks that haunt the landscape of the aging process. These ancient rocks remind me that life has cycles of coming into being and fading from existence. My own life will exhibit this same cycle, as will yours. Thus, a rather practical question arises in my mind for us to consider: Have you prepared your memorial/funeral instructions for your family? There are two discussions to be had here: Do we plan our own service, or do we leave the ritual entirely up to others to plan and execute? Arguments can be made for either option. If we plan our own service, it is more likely to reveal much more about what has been important to us in our lives as well as what we want shared about our self-understanding. On the other hand, planning the service can often be part of the grief work of family members as they craft a service in memory of us. They need to tell stories, share tears and plan our parting ritual as a critical part of their own letting go process. There is no right answer on this one, I can tell you, after years of counseling parishioners on the topic. This is a highly individualized and personal decision.

One of the most difficult funerals over which I presided as a pastor was for a pair of sisters whose very rigid, hard-nosed, judgmental father had died. The daughters were bewildered at how to go about memorializing a man they did not like and who had been a cruel and vain father. He left no notes or guidance about his service and how he wished to be remembered. Yet the daughters knew his colleagues, whom they believed were unaware of this troubling side to him, would also be in the room. The man was well respected in his military officer world.

So I sat with these two women for hours, discussing words appropriate to say and not to say. In the end, I am sure the three of us failed everyone in the room, the daughters as well as the friends because the service ended up being tedious and dry, without life or joy or passion, much like the man in the coffin. The lesson I learned from this experience is this: Even the worst among us needs to speak up about how we want to be remembered.

I fall into the category of people who wish certain pieces of music to be played and poetry to be read at my service. I also have left instructions about cremation and where I would like to have my ashes scattered. I have set up my preferences in my legal documents in order to aid my daughter, who is my executor, when she is planning my service. My decision in the end combines both options: I've left some instructions for things I would like to have happen during my death rituals, and then my daughter can also plan the service as she wishes. I do urge those of you who are reading this book to have this conversation with your family members. Do you want to let them know about your favorite music, or who you would like to say some words about you? Perhaps you have a favorite poem or scripture you would like to have read by a granddaughter or grandson. Whatever interest you have in the shape and tone of your memorial or funeral service, leave some instructions. This takes enormous pressure off the family.

Some seniors find this idea of preplanning their service to be difficult. Others tell me they are willing to have the discussions but have had trouble with their next of kin who do not wish to discuss the topic. The hesitancy can be on both sides. Negotiate the issue if at all possible. It's a "must do" ritual. This conversation aids our family members with the realization that they *will* lose a parent or grandparent, etc. at some point.

This brings to mind another important issue seniors must face. Have you had your will, your Advanced Directive and your DNR (do not resuscitate) documents drawn up? Is your executor chosen? Have your valuables been allotted where you want them to go? Frankly, I am astonished at how many of my senior friends have not dealt with these vital decisions. It's as if preparing these documents will actually cause their deaths! Too much superstition hangs around this issue, for sure. But I can tell you this: We will all die, with or without our documents in place and having them prepared makes things much easier for our loved ones. In so many cases these legal documents have the power to abort family squabbles and court fights. For more seniors than you can count or imagine, this issue has become a sorrowful one as grieving families have become caught in an unintentional legal web.

My reverie about the more tedious details of my mortality comes to an end when I walk away from the balladeers. Enough of that for now!

Wandering among the standing rocks in the stone circle, I reach out and touch some of them as I pass by. They feel solid and strong. I notice that other members of our group are making the same gestures, caressing the rocks, while yet others snap photos or simply sit beside one of the standing icons on the soft, moist earth. No one is talking. An unspoken agreement arises among us that this space is a sanctuary of sorts and talking would be sacrilegious. Just as I am ready to lean up against one of the rocks as a backrest, the sun bursts through the thinning clouds, turning the entire circle into one of liquid radiance. A photo taken of me shows my face aglow with the golden light that is falling from the sky. Joy saturates my body. I am content in a way that I have never before known, merging my soul and body with the rocks, the sun, the landscape. Time disappears and there is only this moment of complete oneness with nature and the Divine. I am whole in a way that feels new. *I am home.*

David said one day this past week, "You cannot enter any world for which you do not have the language." At this moment, standing by this powerful rock in this ancient stone circle in England, as myself, breathing, grinning, a new phrase inserts itself into my lexicon: *rhapsody of nature.* This moment and space is a rhapsody. My body is a song. The earth is a melody. Life itself is a symphony of sounds and sights, smells and tastes. I am truly alive!

Why has it taken so long for this experience to occur in my life? Not until we become aware that life is transient and can expire at any moment do we have access to this moment of recognition that the most precious gift we have is also butterfly-wing fragile, thin and beautiful! Just as surely as I am alive at this moment, the certainty remains that I will also die. The Wisdom Years begin with the acceptance of this truth and accepting a new language for ourselves: *the language of letting go and building a new inner home.*

Our poet leader sends a silent signal that our time with these sacred stones has come to an end and we must return to the farm for our final evening together. I am both sad and exhilarated at exiting this holy space. The return journey to our retreat space found most of the group in a quiet, almost meditative mood as we rocked along in our vehicles through the winding lanes of the English countryside.

Out of the window of my cottage the next morning, I see our vans pull into the parking lot. My exquisite week of poetry and exploring the inner vistas of the heart has ended. We load our luggage and begin the journey back to the Manchester airport, the point of origin for this magical time in these lovely green landscapes. Here I will catch a plane to London to begin Pilgrimage No. 3 into the Cotswolds. As I ruminate on the retreat experience, I am content during the drive. Whatever connections I have made with the people in this van are completed. I glance at the faces sitting around me, enjoying the sweet memories I will carry with me. The woman who rode in this van a week ago is forever changed by these seven days in the landscape of the English Lake District and by the words of a master poet. I can see my reflection cast upon the side window; there is a smile on my face. I am simply grateful.

CHAPTER 5:
BREAKING ALL THE VOWS
PILGRIMAGE NO. 2: INTERIOR STORY

All the true vows are the secret vows,
the ones we speak out loud are the ones we break.
—David Whyte

Although every session with David Whyte splashes words over me
like sacramental waters, today's session is the one that will go home
with me, back to my life in Santa Fe. The retreat could easily end
for me today. I have received what I came for. My anguish over the
important vows in my life now has been given a healing balm.

One of my favorite Whyte poems is titled, *All the True Vows.*
Though I have read these meaningful words repeatedly throughout
the years before this retreat, I do not think I ever fully understood
their depth and pathos—until now. As the poet works intensely
with us on the concept of *vow making and breaking*, I gradually
grasp that our lives are a constant rhythm of ebb and flow around
promises. In David's words, "Vows have seasons." For instance,
when we marry we make a vow to love and give fidelity forever.
But more than half of the Baby Boomer generation have broken
that vow and continue to break it in record numbers, even into the
senior years. Some continue their romantic and relational changes
into third and fourth marriages.

When we bring our children into the world, an implicit vow is
made to protect them, love them unconditionally, and guide them
into the fullness of their adulthood. Yet millions of Gen X, Gen Y,

and Millennial offspring will tell you that they feel poorly parented. Vows that were lovingly made have been unwittingly broken.

We make vows to our employers, at least implicitly, to work diligently, creatively, effectively, because we fully intend to cooperate with our colleagues and express our skills through our creative efforts. Yet work places are replete with misguided behaviors, corruption and gossip, from the CEO's office in the Penthouse suite to the mailroom in the basement. Promises are broken daily, some intentionally and others not.

Humans create promises for every conceivable interaction, both implicit and explicit, both significant and casual: from being a good neighbor, to driving responsibly on the highway, to being a respectful customer, to sharing space in a public park, or walking the frisky family dog. Our culture is laced with mostly unspoken vows formed so we will treat one another respectfully during each encounter. Yet despite our best intentions we constantly and consistently break our communal vows simply because as human beings we are so often unconscious of our behaviors. We fall into habitual patterns, forgetting to stay aware of our effect on others. Again, I offer a reminder of the need for mindfulness training for most of us to aid our interpersonal relations.

One of the most pertinent statements David utters comes halfway through his talk this morning, "When we make a vow, we agree to have it broken at some point in our lives." Wow! Stop and read that sentence again! Underline it if need be—this one is a keeper. Once we make a vow, whether it be something vital to our life story like a marriage vow, or something small like keeping our lawn mowed per the HOA rules of our neighborhood, we immediately recognize, usually internally and subconsciously, that this same vow will at some point be broken, either by us or by another involved in the vow with us. Vows can never be perfectly kept. Why? Humans do not operate like robots. We are fallible creatures, and our promises come with loopholes, conditions, fears and the unknown intertwined inside them. So as I begin to unravel my vow story for you, I invite you to join me while considering your own response to the making and breaking of the crucial vows in your life.

When David completes his talk this morning, I bolt from the room, ignoring the socializing going on with the rest of the participants. Morning tea will just have to wait today! Heading for my cottage so I can write in my journal the myriad of thoughts swirling in my head, I am close to tears. This session explodes my thoughts about several deeply held vows with which I have been struggling since retirement. Prior to this session with David Whyte, I have had no idea how to define and resolve these issues for myself. I just know I am locked into an existential battle over vows I made long ago that express who I am as a person. I have been unable to see my way through the psychological or emotional maze of the vow-breaking steps necessary to move into my Wisdom Years. Now, for the first time, there is a glimmer of hope for my desire to change directions in my life. I offer you my confession.

First, there's the church. You may have detected by now that my life has included a strong commitment to Christianity and service in a church community. I am currently a retired, ordained Presbyterian clergywoman. However, by the time I join the poetry retreat, I have already, at least internally, begun retreating from formal religion, the Church, following quite closely in the footsteps of Rev. Barbara Brown Taylor. Her book *Leaving Church* came with me on my pilgrimage into the deserts of Arizona with Cleve. One night in my tent with the winds howling all around me, I completed reading Taylor's book, grateful that someone else has walked this path before me. Someone else has struggled mightily with her ordination and commitment to the traditional church, just as I am doing.

Before I came to England for this second pilgrimage, I had been quite distressed over whether to continue active participation in the Church. Having attended services in various denominations, I could no longer find a home in the rituals, the teachings, or the worship practices. I attended faithfully, struggling mightily to remain inside my ordination and faith tradition. But every time I attended a worship service, I left angry or bored.

As I began to share my struggle and angst with friends who are also ordained, both male and female, I learned that some of them are going through the same process. As a former professor of Religious

Studies at the University of Oklahoma, I have long considered myself to be somewhat unorthodox in my theology. I wanted my religious practices to be shaped and formed by a more profound and personal spirituality. The contemporary church did not currently offer this to me, in my experiences as a worshipper.

Several years ago, the theology of my faith tradition began to severely fail me in its ability to speak truth to my lived experience. I began to perceive the Church as irrelevant to my life. The anointing of the compassionate and dedicated Pope Francis helped to console me for a while, so I pushed myself harder to stay within the bounds of my church life. But soon I became discouraged again. In frustration, I simply quit. I have joined the ranks of the disenchanted Baby Boomers who are leaving in droves the formal and traditional church. With a jolt, I realize that as surely as I sit here, I have just broken, internally at least, my long-cherished vow with my institutional religious commitments.

The wrestling match with my relationship to my faith has been as intense as Jacob's with God's angels on the ladder to heaven (or so the mythology goes). Finally, I realize that it is my ordination that is creating the crisis within me, not church itself. As a female clergy person who began her ministry in Oklahoma, the fight to become ordained was long and difficult. In the nineties, sexism was rampant and vicious toward women being ordained and serving as leaders in the Church. The scars from that lengthy process still mark my soul. Thus surrendering my role in the Church as a shepherd/leader does not come without a price to my very self-understanding. Vows are taken when one is ordained. Deep vows. Intentional vows. Sitting in my room that night in a remote farmhouse in England, I realize that I must let go of all of it: my belonging to the Church, and my role as a servant in the Church. I must break one of the most meaningful vows of my life: my vow to serve the people of God as their pastor. I can no longer wear my robes and stoles as a representative of the Church and keep my integrity.

This realization thrust a stabbing pain into my heart. But it is time. At this point I have no idea what the consequences of this decision will be or even how all of this will play out in my life. I just know that it is time to break this vow to the Church, its theology and practices, and to my ordination. It is now time for me to surrender this piece of my institutional life to which I have been profoundly attached. This does not occur without tears and anguish of soul, I can assure you. As of now, I have not yet sorted out how to renegotiate this vow for myself. Where will I now find meaning, community, and commitment in my life? Vows can be broken (and many should be), but they must be replaced with some promise that serves the deeper purpose contained within the original vow. In my case I will need to discover a sense of service and connection that means as much to me as did my work in a religious community.

Many seniors do struggle with breaking the vow to their chosen careers and letting go of the way they identify themselves during the professional years of their lives. Within Western society we are identified by what we *do*, not who we *are*. Thus to surrender our identity via retirement and aging does not come easily for many if not most of us, male and female. Yet it is inevitable that we must accept this "letting go" of our identity as employed persons. At some point, we are no longer the teacher, the factory worker, the carpenter, the CEO, the attorney, the district manager, the law enforcement officer. At some point we really are too old or too unhealthy to work in the institutional world!

A recent episode on the Netflix series of "Grace and Frankie" has Saul wrestling with his own retirement; the issues in the story are quite authentic. If all of our lives we have been known as "somebody" by what we have done with our creative skills, then to stop doing our work leaves us begging the question, "Who am I?" As retirement was urged upon Saul, he did not react well because he did not know what he would be unless he was an attorney at the office every day.

A friend shared recently a story about her sister retiring and then plummeting into a deep depression over the loss of her status, identity, and sense of purpose. For days on end, she mourned the loss of her work and her identity. The woman has not yet recovered, and her family is beginning to be concerned about her well-being.

To release our institutional life, for so many seniors, becomes a trial by fire. Yet if we don't break the vow ourselves, it will be broken for us by the institutional world, our bodies, our family, or even our death. At some point, the pressure to leave our work and our life callings will become necessary. So I ask again: *How do we understand and interpret the breaking of our institutional life vows?* The means of letting go is not hidden but is right before us: We *actively* make the decision to break this vow, release our professional identity, and move ahead into the Wisdom Years deliberately and intentionally before this decision is forced upon us. *Adapt and change!*

Realizing I have missed lunch with the group, I cease the intensity of my reflection to begin munching on an apple and some almonds. This break gives me a chance to stare out the window of the little cottage and ponder what lies ahead. I know what is required of me at this point. The clarity I feel right now is exhilarating! Inhaling deeply, I release the knot in my chest. Done! The "letting go" process of my institutional life has begun.

Now it's time to take on one of the most intimate of institutional vows: my vow as a mother. Now, you might ask, "How in the world do you see being a mother as an institutional task?" But if you focus on the question with some relative objectivity, being a parent *is* part of our institutional life. We call it family which is the oldest institution in human society. I have come to know that for the sake of my eldest daughter, it is time to "un-mother" her and break the vow I made to her when she was born.

This middle-aged woman has had a tough life, though mostly of her own choosing. She is strong-willed, intelligent, quirky, and creative. But the choices she has made throughout her adult years about relationships, where to live, with whom to share life, and how to spin her own web of self-interpretations have netted her a troublesome life story. As my firstborn from a marriage that ended in divorce, I engaged in typical Baby Boomer patterns, like trying to salvage my daughter from the consequences of her parent's divorce, and her own decisions about how to respond to growing up in broken and then blended families. None of this went well for her. As a result, by the time she is in her mid-forties, she is emotionally confused and not very independent. I have carried the guilt of this reality for years because I am quite aware that I broke the parenting vow to provide a safe and loving environment for my daughter during her developing years.

As I write in my journal about all the years of struggles I have had over my feelings for this wayward offspring of mine, I break into full-fledged weeping. Thankful my roommate is not in the cottage with me, I push on through my tears to keep writing. My guilt, my frustration, my presence, my absence. Over and over again, I have longed to repair the damage done, all the while knowing deep down inside me that the daughter of my womb needs to do this inner work for herself.

Over the years I have created multiple tactics to fix this situation. First, I was committed to making sure both of my daughters had options for their lives that I did not have in my life as I grew up. Long committed to making sure both were independent, strong women as they came to adulthood, I expressed in my mothering the raw feminism of my generation of women, as we became college-educated professionals in our own right. (In those days Baby Boomer women were, of course, rescuing themselves from the stories their own mothers had to live.)

I longed for my daughters to experience life-changing experiences, unlike my own story. I wanted them to have a chance to become confident, courageous, smart, and successful. Thus, every decision I made on behalf of my children had to do with this dream and desire for them. What I never considered was whether they wanted these options or not. However well or poorly I parented, my longing as a parent failed my firstborn, for sure.

Pulling the blue and yellow speckled yarn afghan over my legs as if I feel a chill invade the room and my heart, I quietly, inwardly break the mother vow. I must let her go. It's time for my beloved first-born daughter to write her own story. I can no longer be her guide, her mentor, or her friend (if I ever was). I have to allow this compassionate and confused adopted-by-Britain daughter of mine to stumble and struggle through her own story so she can grow strong enough to shape her own life. I am almost seventy. I will not be on this earth forever. If I don't do this now, then she will never have a life of her own and will always be dependent on others for her happiness and livelihood.

When I return home, my vow will be to attempt to have a conversation about all of this with my daughter, though I have tried this before without much success. My better option is to write her a long letter about all of my insights and new promises. Hopefully this will prompt the conversation we should have had long ago. The connection between adult children and parents can be complicated and entangled. So finding the best method to communicate such issues is often as difficult as having the conversations themselves. But this does not mean we should avoid or excuse ourselves from this process. Better to muddle through than to miss the opportunity altogether to let our children know that we have grown up enough to allow them to be adults. An amazing and necessary insight!

My struggle now is finding balance in this decision: *How do I love and stay present with my daughter while no longer rescuing her from herself?* I see difficult days ahead for the two of us. We have a long history of familial patterns that we created over the years, shaping the relationship between the two of us at this point in our lives. I have to help her as well as myself to navigate this new vow to "un-mother" her and at the same time become a caring partner to *her* life story. Another deeply held vow must be broken and a new one refashioned. Such intense work is this!

Parenting for Baby Boomers has been easy and successful for some—yes. But frankly, in my world of the Elderlies, I know so many parents who have a troubled child or grandchild somewhere in the mix of the family system. I have listened to story upon story of the anguish and heartache of these parents or grandparents as they confess to having a child in their family who has been unable to leave the nest successfully—offspring who have either moved back home with parents or are living in some wretched situation outside the family circle of care. This pattern now spills down into the Millennial generation with younger Baby Boomer parents and grandparents. So many seniors I know share poignant tales about these young adults who are lost souls in today's demanding world. Are any such situations present in your life? What have you done to rectify, repair, and celebrate the offspring who have troubled stories? What vows need to be broken and remade within your own family?

To add to the complexity of daily life for families embroiled in life transitions, Millennials have begun a troubling pattern of leaving the nest for a trial run at life, either college or first a job or even military service, only to return to their childhood home as they fail to leap successfully into adulthood. Often on my Facebook page, I see a random comment by Millennials whom I know from my teaching days as they post, "I am adulting today." At first this phrase struck me as humorous, but lately I have begun to realize the quip is a sad report on the status of our younger generation, who see the onslaught of adulthood as onerous and intimidating rather than an adventure, as I did when I exited my parents' home to begin my own life journey.

My spouse and I often discuss how things were when our generation of young adults left home for our first job, or college, to marry or even join the military. When we moved away from home, we left for good. The reality was understood on both sides of the fence—we are adults now, not expected to return, and not even particularly welcome back into the nest. Both parent and child were ready for the healthy accomplishment of the "empty nest." But this pattern is no longer always applicable in today's societal structures.

Piled on top of this social incursion into our expectations for how life will unfold for seniors are the grandchildren that so many seniors are now raising or financially supporting. In their sixties and seventies many older adults find themselves rearing the children of their children, while lacking the energy and often the resources to perform this task effectively.

A close friend just admitted to me this week that he is providing childcare for his two-year-old grandson each day to help save this expense for the parents. My friend is in his mid-sixties and tired. He is tied down every day, unable to enjoy the benefits of the freedom of his own retirement. His wife is still employed because they need insurance. The situation is difficult at best.

Another friend is raising her sixteen-year-old grandson while holding a full-time job. She is in her sixties, single and feels exhausted most days. For her life seems empty at one level and too full at another. Such tales are all too frequently the case among seniors. *Another social vow is broken: Our children will raise their children.*

The familial vows among parents, children, and grandchildren are precious and sacred. We are family. We belong together. We are best when we love and respect one another. Yet negotiating life as family in the twenty-first century demands mature psychological and emotional skills, while the stresses and strains of modern life crash in upon us. Living as retirees while at the same time drowning in family complications can bring stress and depression. Vows have to be broken and refashioned in families just as with other institutions in our lives.

In this moment of reflection I surmise how timely David's advice is. We desperately need to become aware of the vows we have made within this institution of family, break the ones that no longer serve the greater purpose, and create new vows based on the life stages we all now inhabit. Promises guide all families, whether spoken or unspoken; they reside intrinsically within our family structures. Ferreting out these vows in order to examine them for their benefit to our lives can be trying with aging parents and grandparents. Vows can become expectations taken for granted among family members, which, in turn, invalidate the intention of a vow. This reality can set in motion ill feelings and behaviors. It is up to us, those moving toward our Wisdom Years, to be brave enough and smart enough to name our familial vows and renegotiate them when necessary. We cannot expect the younger members in our clan to do this for us. To be wise is to recognize and act upon this aspect of relational life.

If you need an example of the breaking and remaking of vows within family life, I encourage you to see the film "Love Actually." This delightful movie contains a collection of family stories played out with a brilliant cast, fantastic writing, and touching vignettes. My spouse and I watch this film together every Christmas just to remind us of our family vows and connections, the shared reality of our common pain and joys, and the complications of sharing our days with people we love.

Soon, I hear the call from the guides that it is time to prepare for our afternoon trek. The vans are humming outside my window. Throwing a scarf around my neck that I bought as a souvenir, I grab my raincoat and run for the door. We are given choices for this jaunt.

I have chosen to spend my time in William Wordsworth's home and the attached museum. Having read some of his poetry prior to the retreat, I developed a respect for his love of nature that matches my own. From the poet himself, "To me the meanest flower that blows can give thoughts that so often lie too deep for words."

Other retreat participants have chosen to visit the home of Beatrix Potter, author of several children's books, but most popularly *Peter Rabbit*. I sense the excitement of the women in the discussion we share as we travel to our various literary venues for the day. For this particular outing, I end up in a van with only females, which creates a vivacious chatter about our jaunt.

As I wander in the gardens that surround the Wordsworth museum area, I feel pulled back into the past by the story of this poet who shared life here with Mary, his beloved wife, and various others, including Samuel Coleridge, who joined them from time to time. I wonder about the vows these three made and broke over the years they knew each other.

Wordsworth wrote some of his most potent poetry in the dark, low-ceilinged spaces of Dove Cottage. When the guide leads us through the miniscule rooms, I shiver from the chill in the air because there is no heat in the house. I was touched by the thought that Wordsworth himself stood right where I am now standing. For me, being in the presence of a poet is far more fetching than meeting someone who is an actor or musician, sports figure or politician.

Staring through a tiny smudged window in the kitchen of the Wordsworth home, I form an interior promise to halt my tendency that allows my daily routines to interfere with the passion I have long held. I vow to resume writing my own poetry. A wash of pleasure fills me to my toes. What a day this has been!

When we return to our quarters after the day's adventures, the smells wafting into the dining area from the kitchen are so enticing that I begin to anticipate dinner with much more interest than usual. Our group converses with high energy, everyone sharing various impressions of the day as they down rich dark ales, a tasty red wine, or simply an Elderflower spritzer (my favorite). Our meal comes out hot, delicious, and very welcome. Roast mutton with colorful root vegetables, a hearty fresh-from-the-garden green salad, and a tasty British pudding (dessert) fill the buffet. But it is the piping hot homemade herbal bread with a pat of locally churned butter that we rush to put on our plates, playfully competing to see who will be first in line.

An hour later, sated and feeling drowsy from the warm food and flowing wines, conversation softens into a hum around the room. I pardon myself from my table of colleagues and plot my escape to return to my room so I might continue writing in my journal. It is time for me to face a tough challenge: The third set of vows I must break. The vows sealed inside my marriage.

Before you become alarmed, the answer is a resounding, "No!" I am not returning home from this pilgrimage to divorce my spouse of over thirty-six years. However, some of our marriage promises made so long ago also need to be broken and renewed. Tom and I inhabit a second marriage, with thirteen years between us in age. We formed a blended family when we married, putting together my two daughters (whom we reared together) and his two older children who were already out of the nest. Because the age gap between my children and his is about a decade, the children bonded easily and quickly. No one was threatened by the marriage alliance.

The early years of our marriage were busily spent rearing my daughters and working to launch my career path. Tom had long been secure in his own professional activities as a professor and itinerate preacher. Although I had completed my education and held a job when we married, I still had yet to launch a professional life that really mattered to me. This reality would emerge as my children began to reach high school age. Nothing extraordinary occurred over the years demanding that we disrupt our marriage or our family. We settled into our life together like most blended families, with kids coming and going between the divorced parents. Tom and I paid close attention to our marriage vows in order to make sure we did not become another divorce statistic (more second marriages end in divorce than first marriages). We were determined this one would stick!

When we were first married, our age separation made little to no difference. But as Tom and I grow older, this span of time between us becomes increasingly relevant. I am now almost seventy and Tom is already in his eighties. Intense conversations have started between us as we watch friends go through their own versions of couple agony (nursing homes or death) while still married and in love. We are quite aware that Tom will be in his nineties while I am still in my seventies. This reality could put him in nursing care long before I am ready to leave our home.

The opposite could also become true—that I pass away while Tom lives as an elderly man requiring help from our children. As we face these impending possibilities and have discussions about them, we notice that much about these scenarios is complicated for us. The reality of our age separation affects everything from our finances, to where we will choose to live, to our actual relationship as we age. Recently we witnessed the parents of a close friend experience just such a situation with the husband living independently and the wife barely surviving in continuous care. The stress on the two of them until she died was tragic.

Regardless of how our aging process unfolds, the truth of the matter is that we will face *something* that will break the vow we made years ago to share life together. Death is the inevitable vow breaker in all our love stories. Even if we manage to stay together for many more years, one of us *will* break the vow first and leave the other behind. Coupling creates this set of consequences. No one is exempt.

Snuggled into a huge chair in the living room of my cottage, the fireplace roaring and a cup of hot spicy cinnamon tea beside me, I begin to mentally and emotionally reflect on what vows Tom and I agreed to in our early years that no longer apply and need to be surrendered. First is always the classic shock that comes with couple retirements: Suddenly you have all day every day with this person. How does a marriage withstand the constant presence of the other when for years we have been separated all day most days and often, in Tom's traveling years, for weeks at a time? Since we are both independently minded, to have to include each other in every negotiation made throughout the day becomes a bit daunting, to put it mildly! Thus the implicit vow of our former independent selves must be broken. *It's now time to make a new vow about proximity and privacy.*

Secondly, Tom and I moved to a new town for our retirement years like so many seniors do. This action created for us the need to start over in terms of friendships, interests, connections, activities. Patterns long held between us when we lived in Oklahoma were broken immediately, and new patterns had to be formed. For instance, we were used to exercising every morning before we left for our university jobs. This set in motion the time when we had to rise each day. Our lives during those years were highly structured: up at 7:00 a.m., to bed by 11:00 p.m., and do it all over again the next day. We followed this routine and our unspoken but highly organized roles for years, each of us knowing what was expected of us.

But retirement has cast us into entirely different roles and routines. Time is ours to manage or squander as we wish. We awaken when we are through with our sleep, exercise each day whenever we wish, eat when we are hungry, play as we find ourselves so inspired. Life seems to flow easily and without much stress and strain. But there can be tension in these situations as patterns for sharing space, tasks, and time have to be renegotiated for the couple. Not an easy task to accomplish after years of long-established patterns and habits in the work world.

One of the critical vows couples must pay attention to as they age is their exercise program. Staying fit as we age, at least for most Baby Boomers, becomes a requirement for a quality life. Yet during these years dramatic changes to the body begin to occur to one partner if not to both. A necessary hip or knee surgery, weight gain, changes in blood pressure, back problems, diabetes, heart issues. Whatever begins to fall apart on us immediately affects our lifestyle. One partner finds they can still do yoga or Pilates; the other has to stop. One prefers to bike; the other partner is unable. One spouse wants to play eighteen holes of golf several days a week; the other needs to ride in the cart or cannot go at all. One spouse still has the stamina to climb mountains or take long hikes while the other can no longer engage in such treks. The list of these difficult situations is endless. Whatever separates the pair from shared activities feels like a broken vow when one partner can no longer participate. New vows must be made when our bodies begin to break down.

Last winter I witnessed the longing of my neighbor who wanted to join her husband outside as he shoveled snow and knocked the heavy wet stuff off their trees. But her foot was broken at the time due to her osteoporosis, and she dared not venture outside. The *vow of togetherness* simply to play in the snow is broken. While this may sound insignificant to a long-term marriage, it is not when this sort of thing begins to occur daily. One person in the relationship continues the active life; the other is forced to slow down. Such realities can break the bond between the couple and cause relentless friction or depression.

After the completion of my four pilgrimages I have deliberately chosen to become a walker. I still continue to hike whenever possible, but walking is something I can do every day with Tom. We have both kept our yoga, prayer, and meditation routine for twenty years now, another discipline we are able to share as we age. Tom can no longer hike with me into the mountains or backpack. But he can do yoga, walking and biking, so we have adapted to our physical realities and our age difference using these exercise forms together. Then, when I can find a friend ready to go camping or hiking, I plan a trip with them to keep that part of my life going.

Some of my senior friends find this to be strange, to plan a trip on my own without Tom. Consternation arose when I announced to some of our friends that I would be going to England without my spouse, on two of my pilgrimages. The older Baby Boomer male is not always open to the woman in his life taking off on hiking treks with another man or even with women friends who hike and camp. But this issue is one Tom and I have had to work out between us to keep the integrity of our own relationship alive and healthy. We have already broken some older vows and made new ones in this area of our lives. It is my assumption that most senior couples have some similar issue to negotiate.

We know one couple who would go dancing every Saturday night. Then the woman developed a form of arthritis that would not allow her to dance any longer. So the husband would invite one of their widowed friends to go with them. His wife sat at their table and watched the two of them dancing, clapping her hands and grinning all the while. The lesson Tom and I have painfully learned as a couple who prefer to stay as active as our bodies will allow: *We must change and adapt to our new reality and make physical adjustments as a couple so that our relationship stays healthy and vital.*

Relational life as we age includes discussion about sexual norms. There is a reason that television and magazine ads for Viagra and Cialis are targeted at the over fifty generation of men and women in relationships. Between aging lovers and married couples, the mores have completely changed. We are living longer, and we are living healthier. Thus, intercourse and intimacy continue to be a desired option for many couples as they age. However, as our bodies change, so do our sexual needs and abilities. Some men need testosterone pills; some women need hormone treatments. Sexual dysfunction clinics abound providing assistance for aging Baby Boomers couples who still wish to stay engaged in healthy, intimate lives.

Vows that affect intimacy become key to a quality relationship for couples in their retirement years. Some vows have to be broken due to changes in health and physical capacities, creating frustration and depression for some. For others, the freedom of retirement releases a newly found sense of romance and excitement. Couples can and often do discover new and exciting connections between them as they begin the dance of aging with joy and a sense of fun. Discovering fresh ways to be sexual as we age can offer a renewed sense of passion and touch. As we grow older our intimacy vows lead us into depths of relationship to which we had no access when we were young and immature. Pleasure in each other as simply people becomes important and appreciated.

Another marriage vow that requires change and adaptation for Tom and me concerns our financial health. Because we both came from former marriages and were single for several years before our marriage, we were comfortable handling our own money independently. Once we married we kept our funds separate until my daughters were grown and out of the home. At that point we mixed our salaries, each of us taking a particular role in handling our common monies. I managed the household accounts and monthly bills. Tom handled our taxes and the finances for our small consulting business. For years, we did things this way, and there was never any conflict over money. But in retirement things have drastically changed for us. We closed our consultation business, our accountant handles our taxes, and there is no other income other than retirement funds. I continue to manage our personal accounts. Tom's work with our financial folio has virtually finished. Thus, I find that I am constantly concerned that Tom stays in the loop for handling our funds in case something happens to me.

Several of our friends have died, leaving their spouses (usually a wife, but not always) ignorant of all the intricacies of the couple's financial life. A younger Baby Boomer friend told me the story of her sister who went through a financial trauma of this sort. The sister's husband died suddenly of a heart attack while he was out fishing. They had owned a series of small businesses across the state of Texas. The husband had never included the wife in the details of the business; she had never asked. All too quickly, she had the entire company on her hands, including employees, payrolls, insurance coverage—all of it.

My friend had no idea how much money she had or whether she even had enough to live on into her retirement years without her husband. She had never worked outside the home. Her days became a blur of attorneys, tax accountants, managers, and travel to each business site. It took her years to settle all of the affairs and decide whether she wanted to keep the businesses running or not. In the end, she became quite a manager along with her youngest son. Between the two of them, they actually grew the business, and it is now highly successful. She has sold her portion to her son so that he has a livelihood for his new family, a wife and a baby girl. This is a success story, but all situations like this do not go this well. This story could just as easily have been problematic for my friend's sister. To keep one partner in the dark about a couple's financial welfare as we age is completely unconscionable. A critical vow between partners and couples becomes necessary for seniors: *the vow to affirm that each partner is cognizant of the couple's finances and knows how to move on alone when this becomes necessary.*

And then there are the seniors who remarry later in life. Money issues become astonishingly complex for these couples. Separate wills?

Grown children? Inheritance issues? Properties? Portfolios? Who are the executors? Such matters take hours of time and discussion to sort out, creating the need for some fairly hefty vows to be carved into the financial picture of the couples involved. If you fall into this category, have you dealt with the issues inherent in such situations so that your families do not have to come to blows? An extended family member is currently aiding with a father who needs assistance while dealing with stepsiblings who are fighting every decision being made. Taking care of the financial vows prior to the days we need care is no insignificant matter.

As I plunder the shape-shifting of lifelong vows, I wish to share with you one last vow that requires our attention: *the vow of friendship*. As an introvert, I have very close and personal friends. However, as a woman who has been formerly a public speaker, I enjoy a wealth of friendships that are not in my immediate circle yet are people I care about. Since Tom and I moved away for our retirement years from the town where we were residents for over three decades, we left behind a community of connections. We knowingly and intentionally exchanged this beloved community for the reality of being forced to make new friendships in Santa Fe. At one level, this has been exciting—new faces, new stories, new experiences. At another level, we have felt the loss of love and shared stories from long-time friendships.

Because we moved away, I have been forced to reassess my connections and commitments to friendship. Several of our closest retired friends have made the same decision—to move closer to grandchildren, or to some long-coveted and exotic location for retirement. So many of our professional colleagues headed to the East and West coasts. We realize we are likely never to see them again, except for the Internet. In the end these moves force dramatic changes in our senior friendships, even with our digital capabilities. In the case of some of our friends, their choice to move away from their long-term home to a new environment has created loneliness and regret. Some seniors who left their institutional home base have actually returned because they were unable to find meaningful connections in their new town or city. I have heard this story more than once or twice!

Other close friends have simply faded away as they have become engrossed in the lives of their children and grandchildren or have developed new interests that do not include me. Many of my friends have begun to travel frequently and all over the world, such that I seldom see them. All of these changes have set in motion for me an intense reflection on *friendship* as I find myself moving toward my Wisdom Years. I realize I must remain open and even seek new friendships for my well-being. Connections are absolutely necessary for living quality senior years.

Likewise, health issues change friendships as we age. One dear friend who lives far from us in Georgia has developed Alzheimer's. Though we chat with him on the telephone from time to time, we are losing him. Every day we grieve the loss of this relationship. Has this situation happened to you? Even locally, as our friends age and physical issues become a nagging part of life, I often feel as if I am losing these special people piece by piece, day by day. The absence of their presence in my life leaves me with a feeling of sadness that has begun to live more and more frequently inside my heart. Certainly at our ages Tom and I have already lost several friends to death. Being a senior requires accepting death and loss all too often. Funerals and memorial services are no longer rare occasions—not an easy task assigned to us as we age. Again, courage is required when illness, loss, and death are not only common; they are to be expected.

Since I have deliberately set myself on a course for transformation within, this will inherently change whom I wish to befriend. Friends I have long known will fade away as others come closer to my center of connection. Seniors often have friendships with people for decades. I have some of those in my life. One of us will bury the other. But my senior years will also hand me new friendships with interests closer to those I have as I adapt to my age. (For instance, I wish to cultivate a set of friends who like to do the walking tours that I have become fond of doing, especially after my walk in the Cotswolds.)

The continuous ebb and flow of the unpredictable stream of life within our senior years that includes moves or deaths or a change in interests urges us to release some of our most cherished friendships on the one hand, while we create new vows of friendship on the other. Friendships are not exempt from this process any more than any other pattern of life in which we find ourselves. *Relational changes will occur, whether we cooperate with them or not.*

There are multiple examples of vows that I could add to the list I have shared. In no way is this list exhaustive, as I have written it. I have simply selected some basic vows I need to consider when I return home: my institutional life commitments, including parenting, my role as a spouse, and friendships. I encourage you to consider what your own vows are and which ones need to be broken and reworked, or permanently released all together. What new vows do you wish to make? The point is this: Life is a process of making and breaking vows, either deliberately or unintentionally. All vows will be broken at some point in our lives, David reminds us. If we can just become aware of the vows we have made, we might then be able and more willing to surrender those vows that no longer work for us. First comes awareness; then comes release. Only then can we gain access to this process of intentional aging and begin the enchanting journey into our Wisdom Years.

If we take our outdated and well-worn vows with us into our aging process, I suspect we will discover that our Wisdom Years have become elusive, replaced by years of disappointment and frustration. Wisdom Years vows need to be fresh, alive and current to this phase of life, to aid the purpose and energy required for formulating a quality life in our later years.

To complete my sharing of the most important internal aspects of this pilgrimage with David Whyte, I offer you a sentence he spoke on day four of the retreat, "The person you are about to become is always a stranger to you." This statement captivated me and offered up an insight to my own story that I have never before considered. I *am* becoming a stranger to myself as I commit to and execute these four pilgrimages. The reason is that I have intentionally set out to change myself and my life patterns. Therefore, as I open myself to the possibilities offered by the pilgrimage rituals themselves, I set in motion the reality that I will change—forever! The person who left Santa Fe to come to England will go back a stranger to herself.

Becoming a stranger to ourselves in the years when we instinctively want to claim confidently that we know ourselves demands a new self-orientation, a sense of risk, and a trust in our ability to handle our inevitable vulnerabilities. Living with mindful reverence toward becoming a stranger to ourselves calls forth in us a calmness and beauty of soul if we allow this possibility to occur.

CHAPTER 6:
THE COTSWOLD WALK
PILGRIMAGE NO. 3:
THE EXTERIOR STORY

On one level wisdom is nothing more profound than an ability
to follow one's own advice.
—Sam Harris

Crafted from dark, heavy wood, the pews are straight-backed, hard, with a narrow seating space and no comfortable cushions as in modern churches. Clearly the artisans who built these pews followed strict instructions from the priest or bishop who commissioned the seats. It is surely true that the worshippers were *not* to be comfortable, nor were they to sit for long periods at a time. Better that these penitent sinners should be bent down on the kneelers with heads bowed and hearts contrite. I pondered all of this, like Mary when she was told she would have a child without benefit of a husband. What would it feel like to be a participant of the faith in this twelfth century remnant when it belonged to the Roman Church? In the confessional of Hailes Church in Gloucestershire, England, lingers quietly the echoes of stories one might want to hear.

Now in the twenty-first century, this sacred space is empty save for Joann and myself. Musty smells rise from the dampness of the stone floors and walls; the worn prayer books rest neatly in their slots. Uneven grey stones form the aisle, rounded by ruts worn into them from thousands of footsteps treading toward the altar to accept the wafer and wine.

Intricate scrollwork inscribed onto the front of the pulpit catches my eye as I wonder about the peasant who might have carved these shapes into the nondescript stone. Was he devout or simply working for wages? Arches grace the various corners of the room, generating an aura of ancient holiness. Faded frescos of various saints cling as residue etched onto the pale masonry walls, a reminder that this building, though currently used by local villagers, belongs to a vanquished past.

Repeatedly, in village after village, Joann and I locate ourselves by three signals of civilization: the church, the pub, the manor house. These remnants of medieval England greet us each day as we arrive tired but euphoric into our next resting place. We almost always come first to the local Anglican Church, usually perched on the outside of town close to the Manor House. Each one is quite similar in architecture both inside and out. I feel like a guest as we visit the first few of these historical buildings, but by the fourth day of the walks, each church building begins to resemble a homecoming to my own story. This walk through the history of England and its churches is a walk through my own story—once reflecting a viable, living breathing faith, now part of my institutional past. The structure still stands here, but it is empty, as long-ago stories resonate through the walls and halls.

We nurture an unspoken ritual, Joann and I. After several miles of walking, we come into these quiet structures with anticipation, to absorb the space around us. First, we drop our daypacks on the bench pew closest to the entrance into the sanctuary. Then, like cats seeking the perfect place to curl up, we each find the pew that invites us to sit down. Usually we sit in silence on different pews. Other days, however, we sit next to each other and whisper (even though no one else is in the room) about our own religious experiences throughout our lives. Resting my feet, weary from the hours of slogging in heavy boots, I sigh deeply and close my eyes.

In the silence of the room I can hear in my head the slow chanting of the Psalms. My nostrils gently inhale the residue of incense that hangs in the air. Sunlight filters through stained glass windows, spilling multi-colored rainbows onto the uneven stone floors. The churches Joann and I visit on these walks through the Cotswolds are vivid reminders of the thousands of souls who have traipsed through them over hundreds of years. Relief and gratitude fill my heart that my newly broken vow to surrender my connection with The Church has not stolen my love for the art and architecture of these places. I *do* love to sit in quiet, empty churches (or synagogues, mosques, or even Buddhist temples), regardless of their age or place or theology or teachings, to enjoy the beauty and reverence I find there, to reminisce about the narratives that have spilled forth in these spaces. For some reason, humans have been able to build exquisite spaces for worship even if they have not always nurtured faithfully the stories or theologies housed within the institutional intentions.

Every village we enter found their beginnings by springing up around these Church of England landmarks as well as the adjoining graveyards, the cornerstones for community and courage among the people who worshipped in these buildings generation after generation. Part of our daily ritual is to explore the graveyards attached to the churches. Joann and I stand quietly, hands folded as we read headstones with dates often scored in the fifteenth or sixteenth centuries. Curiosity invariably overtakes my mind as I contemplate the people whose lives are etched into the worn stones in brief verse. "Beloved Wife and Mother, May She Rest in Peace." Or "He loved his God, his Church, his Family." The markers that create sadness within me are the ones that reveal that a child's bones lie beneath the ground, having lived only five or six years. These are the incomplete stories about which novels are seldom written. As I meander through these memorials to life and death, I am reminded of one of my favorite poems by Thomas Gray, "Elegy Written in a Country Churchyard." These words play through my head:

> Beneath those rugged elms, that yew-tree's shade,
> Where heaves the turf in many a mould'ring heap,
> Each in his narrow cell forever laid,
> The rude forefathers of the hamlet sleep.

The ritual Joann and I coincidently conjure to include village churches in our walking tour becomes the focal point of my third pilgrimage.

I can hear you wondering: *Why would she search for churches after the previous pilgrimage where she broke her vow with the Church?* It's really quite simple: Following the breaking of my *institutional vow* with the Church in my pilgrimage with David Whyte, I am finally free of the clutch the Church has had on my psyche my entire life, beginning in my childhood. Therefore, these buildings with their exposed art and complicated histories call to me as something beautiful to appreciate. I no longer feel emotionally entangled in the rhetoric and theology of the Church. Rather, I can appreciate this historical experience as part of my own story—without attachment and entanglement—something lovely rather than debilitating. My first taste of authentic *freedom* on this pilgrimage begins to bud.

For me this is the first significant break with my institutional life. Breaking with religion could seem heretical to some, but for me this is an institutional release, nothing else. For others, it might be letting go of the family business (like the Italian chef in New York whose restaurant was first established and owned by immigrant grandparents). My spouse often discusses the fact that he had to learn to live without students in his life after teaching for forty years. Regardless of what our various attachments are to our institutional sense of calling, the release is still necessary to be able to enter and engage the Wisdom Years. Letting go of The Church is my attempt at this process. *What is or has been or needs to be your "letting go" project?*

This particular pilgrimage in the Cotswolds of England is a brand-new experience for me. While I have hiked and tramped on trails for over thirty years, I have never before set out to walk from one town to the next without any agenda except simply to walk. I must confess, the idea of a walking tour around strange countryside in a land not my own is a bit daunting. Who does this? Apparently Joann and I do. After a hearty English breakfast at the White Hart Royal Hotel, with our Cotswold maps, daypacks, and hiking poles, we set out on our first morning in a jaunty mood from Morton-in-Marsh. Our goal is to arrive in Stow-on-the-Wold before dark.

Though neither of us knows what to expect from this first day, I do feel a hefty dose of trepidation mixed in with my excitement. All too soon we discover our first task: to learn how to interpret the maps! Though we have both studied the maps in preparation and read the often-confusing instructions prior to beginning our first walk, translating from paper to the pathway under our feet becomes quite a challenge. Laughing out loud I look up to see a street sign with an arrow pointing to the crosswalk on the pavement. Right above the arrow is the silhouette of an elderly couple. The meaning is quite clear. For someone on a pilgrimage to acknowledge her seventieth birthday, the irony of this sign is not lost. What a metaphor for beginning this third pilgrimage!

After wandering down High Street in Morton, staring at street signs, and collaborating over the maps, we eventually find our way out of town. Finally, we locate our path cut on the edge of a cultivated field, and my agitation settles down. Here we begin our walk. *Whew! This will not be as easy as I had imagined*, I thought.

The first day out, we find ourselves spending too much time reading and rereading the maps, as we struggle to learn the language for this British hobby of walking. What is a kissing gate? A field gate? How are they different? How often will we be required to use a stile to cross over a fence? What is a tarmac? Oh, and how do we recognize a Ha-Ha (an ornamental ditch crossing a field that acts as a barrier for animals)? A hodgepodge of brightly colored wild flowers lines the Cotswold path, entangled with each other and dancing in the morning breeze. We stop, take pictures with our phones, and move on with a better attitude. Our pleasant mood is short-lived, however.

Bewildered and often frustrated, the first day's walk becomes tiring beyond belief as we struggle to learn the intricacies of walking in the Cotswolds. And as if we need insult added to confusion, the rain begins. Of course! I wonder if the universe knows we desperately want relief from the downpour as an archway of thick trees appears and covers the trail, providing shelter for us. To escape the rain, we huddle under the dense leaves, which helps to cut the cold wetness to a drizzle.

As we shake the water off our backs and orient ourselves, Joann and I realize there are small clumps of Brits huddling together up and down the road under the same row of trees. We can see that they are involved in intense conversations. I try to listen in on the group standing closest to us, only to realize they are discussing "Brexit." This divisive vote has recently occurred, and most British citizens on the walking paths are mired in concern over this political turn in their lives. At this moment I realize that I have arrived in Great Britain during a historical happening. Just at the Brits are taken aback by the fate they have chosen for themselves, I wonder if I will be just as surprised at the outcome of this pilgrimage year, a fate I have chosen for myself? Only time will reveal the answer to all of us.

Walking on the Cotswold path is an exercise of repetition and endurance. Some might even call it boring, but I found the walks charming and inspiring. In Norway, a diversion named "Slow TV" uses a camera set up to record every moment of an ordinary activity for a viewing audience. For instance, one show involves literally watching a train as it travels down the track for miles and miles and miles. Another camera watches a man as he fishes and the slow, tedious hours of waiting for him to make a catch. The most captivating show involves a group of women knitting a sweater. First, they shear a sheep and then they form the yarn for the garment—over eighteen hours of viewing tedium. Or is it?

This unique television series has become increasingly popular in an eerie way as thousands have tuned in to watch time pass in an endless array of monotonous moments. Why would this program become so well liked? The answer seems evident to me: The modern world is moving too fast, with too much chaos and clatter. This Norwegian audience is relearning the art of "taking life slowly."

The Cotswold walk allows me, for nine days, to slow down every moment into an enjoyable sensation of absolute beauty and measured breath. Every day fashions itself into a blend of walking through horse, cow, or sheep pastures, dodging manure, or sauntering along country roads lined with thickly leafed trees. Joann and I wander through countryside so pastoral and peaceful that I am transported into another state of being. The *gift of slow* becomes evident in my psyche as my body fully relaxes and adapts to the daily walks. Surely this is a wisdom lesson about aging—grasping the slow and steady, calm and peaceful pace in our later years when our bodies actually begin to require this of us. Rather than resent having to "slow down," could we perhaps learn to be grateful for the opportunity and gift of this process?

When Joann and I top the various hills on our trail, the view before us resembles a patchwork quilt of various shades of green, deep and dark, light and pale, with the occasional wheat field of golden yellow thrown into the mix. My favorite site is a stunning field of lavender bushes, one of England's exports. The pungent smell and vivid explosion of color set my senses to spinning with excitement. I have seldom seen such a splendid sight—purple as far as my eyes can see. (Purple is my favorite color!) I stop and take time to inhale the fragrances before me. The last time I remember such a vision I was in Kansas standing next to a vast field of sunflowers.

Our most frightening encounter on this pilgrimage comes when a huge—actually massive—male sheep lies down in the gateway where we are supposed to pass. Joann and I look at each other, eyes wide, and I ask, "Who goes first?" She looks at me with a resolute face, "Not me!" So I approach the gate, thinking that I must some-how find a way over the fence. This determined sheep is not going to budge from our path. And I am not of a mind to challenge him. I was not reared in a rural setting, and I know nothing about sheep. This is not the moment I want a lesson about this woolly mammal! But now I have a problem: Going over the tall, wooden fence will not be easily accomplished either. This task looks just as daunting as facing the sheep in my path.

As I study the situation, I notice a slender, blond-headed man standing on the opposite side of the fence watching the two of us with a slight grin on his face. I approach the enclosure with trep-idation. The stranger kindly aids my climb up and over by stick-ing his arm through the fence and pulling me toward him. I almost tumble over the high, white barricade, but I do manage to make it across without breaking any bones. Success! Then we assist Joann. With a profuse thank you, I learn that our hero is on holiday from Switzerland with his wife and two children who are also scouting out the Cotswold walks. We all have a good laugh about the stubborn black-faced sheep that just stares at us while slowly chewing on grass, completely unbothered that he has caused such trauma.

The first four days of this pilgrimage are mostly cloudy, with frequent rain showers, or sprinkle binges that drive us from time to time into the nearest pub. One particularly cold, wet day of walking we find ourselves rounding the corner of a slick asphalt tarmac into Naunton, only to be tossed into a drama that is occurring with a bicyclist who has fallen on the wet pavement. Gathered around him are his wife and friends, all waiting for an ambulance to come and whisk him to a hospital. The disgruntled group is thoroughly frustrated because they have waited for over an hour, and the ambulance has not arrived. We stop to offer aid and encouragement, but quickly discern that we are more of a nuisance to them than of any help.

To escape the gray mist falling on our heads, Joann and I dash across the street into the Black Horse Pub to find warmth and down a hot drink. It's the middle of the afternoon, so no food is available from the kitchen. The young woman behind the bar offers us the privilege of taking off our boots to set them on the heater so they might dry before we head back outdoors again. I forage for something—anything—to eat, and Joann secures a table close to the blazing fireplace. As we settle down to dry out, my eyes search the room for its novelty. I spy a family at another table in a dim corner of the room, huddled together talking in low voices. I study them with interest. What brings people into a pub in the middle of a rainy afternoon? I am still puzzled by this British hobby of "pubbing" at all times of the day. Perhaps this is their way to slow down the day and simply enjoy one another in easy conversation. Might Americans learn this lesson and try to reduce the speed of our frenetic routines?

Before long, our clothes are dry and our boots are manageable again. When one is a walker, rain is not an excuse to halt the journey. Joann and I both understand that we will soon be back outside in the wet to finish our walk to our accommodations in Winchcombe. This will be the halfway point of our pilgrimage and the place where I will celebrate my seventieth birthday.

This walk nets us one of the more interesting sites we see on this journey through the Cotswolds: Sudeley Castle and Gardens. The tomb of Tudor Queen Katherine Parr, Henry VIII's sixth wife, one of two wives to survive the amorous, adulterous King, resides on the grounds. Unlike the other unfortunate wives, at her death Katherine would be buried in a private residence, Sudeley. (As a strange aside, her lost tomb would not be found for many years.)

When I was a teenager, I had been mildly obsessed with the Tudor tales of misogyny, murder, and mayhem. Wandering around the grounds of the castle ruins and the beautiful intact chapel where Katherine offered her daily prayers, I felt a tug on my psyche, pulling me back into the fourteenth century when she lived. What would it have been like to survive in her world? Did she ever ponder the mystery of wisdom and waiting? Every generation has this same dilemma: We all live; we must all face our demise. Some do this better than others. Unlike Anne Boleyn, Katherine's survival with Henry was not a daily threat, though she did have moments when her life was in jeopardy. What happens to the human psyche when life is perilous and threatened? What does the caustic diagnosis of a terminal illness do to our hearts and minds when faced with our impending death?

One of the best books I have read on the matter is a recent release: *It's Not Yet Dark* by Simon Fitzmaurice. I commend this one to you if you too ponder such questions. Such thoughts run through my mind as I meander around among the castle ruins. I suppose turning seventy on this day brings up the reality of my aging in a poignant way, causing me to be reflective about my own birth, life, and death. I suspect most seniors wonder from time to time as we age whether we will be remembered or not. I can remember my great-grandmother. But when I die, the memory of her will be gone. No one else in my family knows who she was. This inevitability of our earthly coming and going brings a shock and sadness to the psyche, doesn't it? Do you ever choose a year in the future when you know you will not be on earth but wish you could be? I often wish I could see the grandchildren of my first-born granddaughter, but I won't be around for that. This sort of realization is the impetus we can use to urge us to practice intentional aging.

Astonishment could not have been more profound as we arrive at our lodging in Winchcombe. The Wesley House on High Street—a place where Rev. John Wesley had stayed in both 1756 and 1779 was simply perfect. Wesley was the beloved Anglican Priest who founded

Methodism. As the porter shows us to our tiny loft room above the restaurant below, I squeal in delight. The name on the door of our quarters for the night is: *Preacher's Room*. Could anything have been more appropriate for me at this point?

Today is my seventieth birthday, July 15, 2016. I have been a preacher for the past twenty-five years of my life. When I return to the States, I will preach my final sermon in Aurora, Colorado, sharing this moment with some of my favorite people on Earth. Cleve and his wife, Nancy, will be in this audience, as will Joann and her husband, Dave. Neither of my pilgrimage compatriots (Cleve and Joann) were aware of my struggle with leaving the institutional church. As Joann and I are unpacking, I glance across the room and find myself so grateful for these days with her because she has been willing to share this pilgrimage adventure with me, without judgment or worry. Our time together has been easy and compatible.

Sleeping in John Wesley's room seems like such an appropriate way to bid adieu to this part of my life story. Wesley is known as the cleric whose "heart was strangely warmed." I knew that "warmed heart" during my ministerial years and now find myself grateful and humbled, even as I leave the institutional life that has nurtured and fed me for so many years. I am deeply relieved that the anguish and anger over this release of my institutional ties with the Church has morphed into gratitude. I am finally at peace with this decision.

My birthday celebration dinner takes place at 5 North Street, Winchcombe, Gloucestershire. We have reservations for 7:00 p.m. The chef is Michelin-starred, my first as far as I know, of this caliber. The meal comes with seven courses and is absolutely perfect. Every bite is delicious. Joann and I luxuriate in the charming atmosphere of the restaurant with its wooden floors, beamed ceilings, and antique furniture scattered throughout the various rooms. Our table is nestled next to a window fronting onto the street where we can peer out at the people walking by on their way to various venues for the evening. The daylight is lovely as it wanes, casting shadows around the dining area. Everything around me feels soft and ethereal. What a delightful evening—an excellent way to turn seventy!

What matters most to me on this day is the ritual acknowledgment of my birth. I notice that many seniors, as they age, forget or ignore this important life marker, feeling as if birthdays make them "feel older." My mother, for instance, did not appreciate her birthday and did her best each year to encourage her children and spouse to ignore the day. However, what I have learned about the reality of birthdays is that we *are* older, whether we acknowledge it or not. So I ask, "*Why not celebrate the day? It's better than the alternative.*"

Birthdays are wonderful reminders of the gift of life, inviting us to renew our vows, challenge our tendency to be sedentary, and encourage us to envision new vistas and adventures for ourselves. Like celebrating New Year's each year with resolutions, I find, as I age, that birthdays become the perfect occasions for these transformative moments. Why not? Life is not over until it's over! How many times am I going to be seventy? Or eighty? Or ninety? Will I become a centenarian? I hope so. Imagine, if you will: one hundred candles to blow out! Now *this* I want to see! Our birthdays are an ideal time to renew our personal vows, those promises we make to ourselves about what we could or should do to make our lives more meaningful.

While reading the book *Sapiens* by Yuval Harari this past year, I came across a statement he wrote that struck a chord with me: "A meaningful life can be extremely satisfying even in the midst of hardship, whereas a meaningless life is a terrible ordeal no matter how comfortable it is." Words of truth and encouragement for all seniors to hear, I suspect.

The day following my birthday, Joann and I take off for Stanton, which is ten miles away. The weather has dramatically shifted at this point—time for short sleeve hiking shirts, rolled up hiking pants, wide-brimmed hats and sunscreen! For me, I feel as if I am back in Arizona with the sun blazing down on me—except for the grueling humidity here that saps my energy.

On this walk through the pastures and hillsides, I am a bit pensive as I find myself remembering my parents. My father made it to age eighty; my mother died at age seventy-four. Now that I am seventy, her early demise becomes an unpleasant reminder that I am moving closer to the same age. One of the striking realities of being a senior is that the closer we come to the date of the death of our parents, the closer we come to our own death. Funny how that happens, isn't it? The world my parents inhabited no longer exists. My father was a young soldier in WWII. My mother carried on her life as a war bride, working and waiting for her husband to return. Their stories are now lost forever in a trunk full of unlabeled photos and mementos. Once we realize we are the next generation in line who will pass away, a sober reality check occurs. We have become our grandparents and our parents. Sometimes this recognition startles me. A generation has passed, and I'm up next!

Isn't it strange that as we age, we find ourselves more consciously remembering our parents? What I wouldn't give to talk to my parents now that I am seventy! Especially my mother. At this stage of life I have so many unanswered questions about her life that I was never conscious enough to ask when I was younger. Like most offspring, I took for granted that my parents would live forever. They were never "old!" They were simply my parents. Then one day they were gone, and there remained no way to ask questions of them. A second awareness: This generation of parents did not easily share their stories with their children. These folks were known as the "Silent" Generation or the "Greatest Generation" depending upon their ages. Many, if not most, of those stories are lost in the obscurities of time and will never be recovered.

This rumination makes me aware that I do not want my own daughters to have so many questions about me after I am deceased, when they can no longer learn about their own mother. For sure, there are events in my past that my children will never be privy to, but I also do not want them left wondering who I truly have been: my values, my beliefs, my stories. To my way of thinking, this is another ritual of the Wisdom Years that should include our children. So how might this be done? Through journals, letters, sharing stories, videos, etc. In this digital age many ways of leaving "bread crumbs in the forest" exist that would provide clues to our children about their parents' life stories.

Have you noticed the increase of interest in ancestry searches and genealogy studies in American families today? Telling our life stories, regardless of format, allows the next generation to recover insights into their own stories and histories. A thread runs through our family memories, like beads on a string, revealing who we are and what mattered in our limited days on earth. Part of our responsibility as seniors is to share our experiences and allow our heirs to know who they are by extension.

By the way, I do fully understand that our children and grand-children are, for the most part, not interested in our stories—yet. This is the occasion for some pain on the part of the Elderlies who long to leave their tracks in the sands of time. Paper and digital trails may be the best we can do for the moment. My encouragement is this: Even if sharing your story on paper or into a video camera seems fruitless, do it anyway. Someday, long after we are gone, our heirs will cherish these memoirs.

My favorite of the small villages visited on this pilgrimage is Broadway. On the road into the heart of the town, we come to an open field where we stop to watch for a few moments the game mysterious to most Americans: cricket. I have *never* understood this game! As we crest the hill into the edge of town we learn that Broadway has two ancient churches, St. Eadburgha's Church that is a twelfth century building, and St. Saviors Catholic, a parish that claims to be over one thousand years old. Following our normal pattern, Joann and I start walking in the direction of both of these sites, enjoying the beauty and uniqueness of each.

In St. Eadburgha's Church I take my normal round of photos, the chancel, the pulpit, the archways, and then I sit down on a wooden pew to soak up the ambiance of this sacred space. When we are in our room in Dove Cottage later in the evening, I write in my journal, "*The church speaks more to me when it is empty and quiet than when it is full of noise and action.*" What an astonishing place for meditation and prayer!

For the first time on this pilgrimage here in Broadway, we spot the famous "thatched roofs" of long-ago Britain, as well as beautifully manicured gardens at the B and B where we are housed for the night. This area certainly lives up to its reputation for representing a taste of historical, quaint Medieval England. But the most pleasant experience is the moment we come across the Crown and Trumpet Pub on Church Street. Joann and I know we have located our special spot for "people watching," one of our favorite pastimes in these Cotswold villages. Locating a table outside, we stake our claim for the space even though the day is hot and sunny (Yes! It truly is!). For the umpteenth time I order fish and chips, along with an Elderflower spritzer. This has become my favorite noonday pub meal on this pilgrimage. We sit lazily for a couple of hours, enjoying the villagers as they stroll by, lethargic from the heat after previous days of damp and cold.

My mind wanders while I sit under the shade umbrella that spares us from the heat. There are several motorcycles parked just beyond the pub patio, shiny, black, and loaded with fancy gear. As my eyes search around the patio space, I locate the couples most likely to belong to the cycles simply by the clothing they are wearing: black leather pants and jackets emblazoned with symbols I don't recognize. Before long they down the last sip of their various ales and beers, and then they amble over to their cycles, separating into pairs to climb onto the mechanical beasts. With ear-splitting sounds, the cycles roar away on some unknown adventure. I envy the freedom of these travelers. Immediately after I have this thought, I plunge into an inner dialogue on freedom.

This third pilgrimage, I realize, is quickly becoming a metaphor about human freedom, in particular, my own. I have planned this trip and come abroad to walk as I wish and will. No one has interfered with my right to do this or my ability to make this trek happen. I am travelling where I wish without bonds or boundaries. I have no responsibilities at the moment but simply *to be in the moment*. Isn't this freedom? Or is it? On our walk from Broadway to Chipping Campden "the transparency moment" occurs as the purpose of this entire third pilgrimage slips into my conscious mind. When this epiphany occurs, I am standing in a wheat field under the blazing hot sun, fully aware and awake.

Joann and I end our trip coming full circle back to Morton-in-Marsh. We are housed in the same hotel, the ultimate expression of quaint, though in a different room on a different floor. At this point I feel at home in this space with its antiquated rolling wood floors and slanted rooms. Heading down to the restaurant for a light dinner, we reminisce about our walks. This has been an amazing venture, one that will live with me for years to come. Quite likely I will be lured back to walk another segment of the Cotswolds, perhaps the Bath area. But there is only one "first time" for such an experience as this. I know the feelings I possess can exist only for this particular moment in time. Inside my heart there is a flicker of sadness at this reality.

Tomorrow we train back to London for our long flight to Denver. I am so grateful that I "took my own advice" (see the epigram) and planned these walks to help me begin to advance into my Wisdom Years. This pilgrimage in the Cotswolds will go down in my memory as one of those lifetime adventures of "bucket list" quality. Never in my life have I been so inspired on a day-to-day basis. Why? Time slowed to a crawl, and I was allowed for nine magical days to live in an alternative dimension of peace and consciousness. Time in the Cotswolds has had no edges or walls. I have been allowed to be, for a short time, a true pilgrim, exempt from ties and boundaries except the eternal pathway before me. My quest for meaning and purpose now begins its slow dawning in my soul.

Chapter 7:
Anonymous Pilgrim
Pilgrimage No. 3:
The Interior Story

With or without him, the moon and the wind
would go on, rising and falling.
The land would keep stretching ahead until it hit the sea.
People would keep dying.
It made no difference whether Harold walked, or trembled,
or stayed at home.

—Rachel Joyce

Harold Fry walked a pilgrimage from Kingsbridge in South Devon to Berwick-upon-Tweed to save the life of his unrequited love. Along the way, he encountered himself through the faces and voices of all those who wandered into his journey. If you enjoy quirky, creative, touching stories, you will want to read about Harold! On my third pilgrimage I accidently (or was it?) came across a book by Rachel Joyce titled, *The Unlikely Pilgrimage of Harold Fry.* I knew nothing about the book and had never before read this author. I picked up the book based on the title alone and stuffed it into my daypack because the setting is England, and Harold is on a pilgrimage.

By the time I finished reading the book, I have also completed my third pilgrimage. Harold and I are busy doing something similar: He walks to save Miss Queenie and thus finds himself. I walk to save myself and thus, also, find my Self. Our separate but similar pilgrimages, walking through some of the same countryside, tell the story of freedom for both of us. I will leave you to enjoy Joyce's book on your own, but if you read my story below, you will know Harold a bit better before you read his story. The clue lies in the epigram attached to this chapter.

I alluded in the previous chapter to the idea that this third pilgrimage offers me an authentic taste of genuine freedom. Now, as an American, educated, professional, white woman, I have known a type of freedom—liberty—all my life, to be sure. I am certainly privileged and blessed with an abundant life. I am not naïve about this. However, most of American citizenry—regardless of financial, racial, social, or gender status—fail to understand the limitations under which we live in terms of our actual freedom of Self. This is why the consumer-oriented lives we lead can easily keep us trapped. More than enough of us believe that what we are able to *buy* and what we actually *have* or *do* determines our freedom, not who we *are* as persons.

Understandably, it takes some philosophical and psychological savvy to actually recognize freedom in its truest form, to think deeply enough about our personal freedom to understand it. For independently minded Americans who believe we can "do what we want to do when we want to do it with whom we wish to do it," the idea that we might not be as free as we think is somewhat puzzling. To some, it is a downright anathema to think this way, given current trends in our society. Before walking in the Cotswolds, I was like you. I assumed, "I am a free person able to do as I choose." And at one level, for the most part, I am that person. I can choose where to live in terms of a town or state, whom to marry, what route to take to the store, what book to read, what to wear, who will be my friends, even my work within reason. In philosophical language this type of freedom is called *liberty.*

But authentic freedom of Self and Soul—*autonomy*—lies deeper and comes at a dear price, usually not one we are always willing to pay. Only in the impending Wisdom Years is it possible to even vaguely recognize the capacity for our most authentic freedom. Please allow me to explain.

As I stand in that golden wheat field outside of Chipping Campden on the final day of walking these thousand-year-old paths—this is the moment I am struck with the insight that frames the foundation for my upcoming Wisdom Years.

The walk today is almost eight miles. The sun is blazing hot, stifling as Joann and I share our final walk. The wheat shimmers like waves, a bright yellow color, matching the sun above me. Sweat runs down my face from under my hat. My arms begin to turn pink and painful. When I started this walk at nine o'clock this morning, my sleeves were rolled down, causing me to forget my sunscreen. An older couple passes me on the trail. She looks miserable. He seems worried about the fix they are in on the rutted, narrow path. They are both wearing the wrong shoes for a walk like this. Crossing the field takes what seems like an eternity, unlike most of the fields Joann and I have trekked. This one is endless.

My mouth is dry. Under this piercing, humid heat, I seriously need a drink of water. The path where I have stopped is so narrow that I wonder if I should not just keep moving along into the trees and shade. Lush plants along the pathway brush against me, creating a sweaty itch on my bare shins. I look back and see Joann some fifty yards behind me. Her head is bent under her dapper little hat as if she is trying to avoid the heat while marching surely and steadily along this demanding trail.

I have two choices as I stand here in the sun gulping from my water bottle: complain or cope. So sucking in a deep breath, I focus my eyes on the beauty around me. For as hot and uncomfortable as I am in this setting, the vista is still lovely—golden wheat, about thigh high, surrounded by hedgerows of dark green that I can see in the distance lining the edges of the field. Pulling my phone out of my pants pocket, I shoot a photo of the massive field of bright yellow. Once this is done, for some reason unknown to my conscious mind, I decide to call my spouse. The call will not go through. Ah, there is no service. I am disconnected from the world. Suddenly, standing in a field in the Cotswolds, I am cognizant of this *moment of transparency. I am an unknown.*

My mind begins to race with the power of this insight. No one here in this immediate space or time knows me. I am alone. Joann is lost in her own world on the trail far behind me. None of my former titles—Reverend, Dr., Mrs., Mom, Amma, Barbara, Skye—matter here. None of the labels that describe me have any significance in this setting: daughter, wife, mother, friend, neighbor, pastor, professor. None of these titles will gain me anything I might need or want. Here, in this time and place, I am fully *anonymous and insignificant.* Like Harold, *it makes no difference if I walk or tremble.* The wheat field, the sun, the wind, the birds calling above, the hard earth beneath my feet continue without me. My presence is unnecessary to the continuation or extinction of any of this. I am one who is simply passing through. My living and my dying are irrelevant in the grand scheme of things. The moment for my distinct existential crisis of aging arrives, completely without fanfare!

I do not recall in my life ever before feeling "anonymous." I have felt ignored or discounted, but never totally *unknown.* The first years of my life I was "Mayfield's eldest daughter, Sue." Then I was a young, inexperienced, corporate wife. Soon, I became the mother of two daughters. Then I became Barbara—the name I chose for myself when I felt like an adult. Next, I was Tom's wife. Time passed and I became Reverend, Pastor Barbara and Professor Boyd. Finally, in the David Whyte retreat I reclaimed a spiritual name I had long held inside my heart: Skye. Naming is how we identify ourselves. All my life I have *belonged* to some person or traditional institution as a way to identify myself, to be known. But never have I felt or understood myself to be purely anonymous. This dancing wheat field in the south of England becomes that *moment of anonymity* for me.

My ego sloughs away and for a few precious moments I am a being, unattached, unfettered, free. Not just free to do as I wish, which is a much more superficial understanding of freedom, the feeling of liberty. Rather, I am freed from being labeled or identified by society or by myself as someone necessary and important. I am anonymous and autonomous, neither more nor less necessary or important than anyone else. I am merely a living creature who is passing through a given time and space on this planet called Earth. I will fade away in due time, but for now in this moment I am fully alive and free because my ego, my identity, my titles do not define my Self.

I cannot be reduced to who I have been, what I have done or what I have been attached to in this life. I am simply a woman walking through a wheat field, as though in some obscure Russian painting, without a name or a place. I am a Being, nothing more, nothing less. Perhaps this is how Eve felt in the Garden for those few moments she had on her own, unattached, pure, holy.

Autonomous freedom is the freedom of being that comes from within one's interior Self. I like to describe this type of freedom by using a metaphor about prison. If I were to be incarcerated, locked away for life, am I still free? If I define freedom as liberty, then the answer is "No, I am not free." However, if I am autonomous in my orientation toward life, guided by the law of my own Self (the definition of autonomy), then I could actually know freedom of Self even while in a prison. I would not need to be defined by the crime I had committed. I could be reformed and transformed into a New Being, fully autonomous. The reason for this truth is that if we do not totally define freedom by our ability to *do* as we please, but rather by our freedom to *be* a whole and conscious Being, guided from within, then we have the capacity to claim our freedom of Self.

In other words, I can resent my imprisonment (the taking of my liberty) and fight against it for the rest of my life, and in some cases this is the wisest thing to do if one is imprisoned unjustly. But I can also choose to view myself as free to live as one who is whole and at peace with Self, regardless of whether I am able to do as I wish. Holocaust prisoners of war who managed to somehow survive the horrific extermination camps speak of freedom in this manner. Some remained free, even while imprisoned. I am utterly convinced this division of understanding about freedom in a society like ours is difficult much before age fifty or sixty (unless one is caught in traumatic circumstances) because our institutional lives have such an intense claim on us.

Another entrance into the Wisdom Years begins with letting go of our need and desire to be known, accepted, included, and titled. The Wisdom Years for seniors are ascertained by our willingness to become anonymous so that our autonomy might flourish. Our institutional years are marked by what we *do* for the given institution that we choose to serve. Our talents, skills, experience, and a bit of luck control our destiny at this point in life, and we become identified by what we do for the group that claims our time and energy. Our status matters. Nothing is particularly wrong with this perspective during the institutional years. Shaping our identity is a critical part of our psychological development when we are younger, providing us with an ability to function well in society.

The Wisdom Years, however, are better established by understanding who we *are*. In other words, the quality of these senior years might best be focused on my *being*, not my *doing*. To nurture ourselves into whole and balanced human beings requires us to *be nothing*, rather than something. Herein lies the deliberate move from the institutional years into the intentional years. In order for this transition in consciousness to occur, we must become aware of how often we think of ourselves as *someone who has done or is doing something of importance or relevance*. Breaking the spell of our own self-importance requires us to execute one of the more difficult tasks of becoming wise ones.

When I gather with a group of seniors who are strangers to me, the first instinct for all of us in order to become acquainted is to identify ourselves to each other by what we have accomplished in the past, in our institutional lives. A litany of credentials flows, as each person tries to establish his or her place in the pack by naming the previous work or career, or the company who employed us, or even the profession to which we belonged. American adult society has a strict ranking system built into it by which everyone understands how important or how insignificant she or he is once it is revealed how the institutional days and years are spent.

My spouse tells me that in his senior male social groups this habit plays itself out when males reminisce in the local coffee shop about the past accomplishments of their professional lives. In senior female culture, we often identify ourselves by how many children or grandchildren we have, and what they are up to as young adults. Younger Boomer women tend to play the same game as their male counterparts, sharing what they do or did in their professional lives, *then* sharing the story of their children and grandchildren. This gives them prestige of a sort.

I am not unaware of how difficult it is to simply let the conversation flow without naming our credentials so others know how important we were in our institutional lives. It takes a great deal of effort to stand in the club, or lobby, conference hall, or even the church narthex and remain anonymous. I challenge you to try to get to know a stranger without telling him or her who you are, without claiming your credentials or without asking theirs. Time how long it takes before this topic arises. Only a few moments at best is my experience. This is *not* easy to do in American social settings! We are not comfortable with anonymity! In fact, we are quite suspicious of anonymity.

But somehow I have come to believe that the heart of the Wisdom Years insists on our ability to let go of the labels that identified us in the institutional years. It is now time to manifest a *sense of being* and release our *sense of duty to doing*. This alternative way of thinking allows us to become more comfortable with ourselves as we are, warts and all. The Wisdom Years invite us to appreciate a different kind of beauty in the wrinkled, splotched, balding, aging, aching bodies we now inhabit. The Wisdom Years call us to make peace with having released our professional lives to live intentional lives. The Wisdom Years require us to change and adapt to what occurs in body, mind, and heart during these years. Aging urges us to release our ego attachments to the past in order to once again become curious, eagerly invested in a fresh creative pattern of being and living in the present.

As a disclaimer, I must say that I am not a champion of making seniors any more invisible than we already are. This is certainly not my aim. From Harold's story comes this sentence, "It was rather that he had passed through life and left no impression. He meant nothing." A feeling of insignificance is certainly not one I desire seniors to have. To feel lost and useless creates turmoil and trauma for seniors. The heart of anonymity is not grounded here. Rather, anonymity is a tool to gain our authentic freedom, our autonomy, our fullness of Self, our wisdom.

There is an appealing grain of truth in Harold's thought. As seniors, if we stay attached to worrying about the impression we will leave behind, or whether we will leave an impression at all, we will never be free to explore the Wisdom Years as a conscious, joyful, free, autonomous and authentic revelation of our True Selves. There is a delicate balance here between making ourselves invisible, versus creating a bold and autonomous Self, willing to speak and live the truth of our wisdom to a world much in need of this without ego attachments.

With this insight, I am calling for a revolution of sorts for seniors entering into the Wisdom Years. Now is the time when our life experiences, our expertise, our wisdom is most valuable to each other, to our families, and to society. What I am calling for is an internal sense of freedom that provides us with the courage to offer ourselves to society as a valuable resource without wanting to be in control of the outcome or our role in it. Most seniors have realized that some event lies ahead which we will not be here to experience. (For me it's living on Mars!) The freedom of the Wisdom Years means that we no longer need to control the future because we have finally learned to live in the present.

In our institutional years we tend to become invested in results and consequences. The outcome matters to us because our egos are invested in whether we are successful or not. If carefully nurtured, the Wisdom Years set us free from this way of thinking. Our ego accomplishments do not need to control our lives when we live as autonomous, mindful beings. We can cherish the surprise and amazement, the mystery and magic of life rather than striving to have a seat at the table of power and status. At this stage of life, we should be comfortable in our skin, even if it is wrinkled! Our sense of adventure and joy at being alive replaces the intensity and stress of the institutional years. The Wisdom Years call us fully into gratitude and courage. We *are* Being Itself.

Do we leave it here? The answer is a resounding "*No!*" I am not asking seniors to "do" nothing as we arrive into this stage of being. Our Wisdom Years, once we have discovered the beauty of living the anonymous/autonomous life, bring us to a new way of "doing" our lives. This applies to any and all of that with which we choose to become involved, be it humanitarian work, a new small business, family caretaking, traveling and exploring, hobbies. Allowing ourselves to find a new freedom within invites us to explore that "bucket list" of activities that has long resided, perhaps secretly, in our hearts. Joy becomes the operative word!

One of the more interesting stories of a public figure making this autonomy discovery has been the change of heart and life of former President George W. Bush. A man who never understood himself to be a painter has become one. His way of describing how he became a painter is spoken in his familiar Texan-ese: "I just had one of those itches. My advice is when you get an itch like that, try to scratch it, especially if you are an old guy like me." Bush is now over seventy years old. I use his story as an example of the ability of one man whose institutional past was completely contrary to his senior years in which he has reinvented himself. He found the freedom within himself to be bold, take a risk, and put himself out there in society with a new offering. He does not claim to be a good painter, just a painter with a heart for what he now loves to do. Whether or not you approved of George Bush as president is irrelevant to this story. He has become an example of one who found his freedom and turned it into a new way of being Himself, an autonomous, anonymous painter. We are never too old to write the next page of our own story.

Chapter 8:
Roots and Rocks

Pilgrimage No. 4:
The Exterior Story

I shall be telling this with a sigh, somewhere ages and ages hence:
Two roads diverged in a wood, and I—
I took the one less traveled by,
And that has made all the difference.
                                          —Robert Frost

Vermont in the autumn—leaves, leaves, and more leaves. Color, astonishing colors, all over the ground, and dripping from the trees. This land is seductively splendid, with dense, brilliant forests, ambling rivers, rushing waterfalls, and imposing boulders—almost like an outdoor playground for nature lovers like myself. Naively I organize this fourth and final pilgrimage to take place in the Green Mountain National Forest, on some sections of the Long Trail, and also within the Moosalamoo National Recreation Area. I have invited Tom to join me for this journey. The plan, with a guide to haul our luggage and transport us each day to our trailhead, is to complete daily hikes arriving at our bed and breakfast each afternoon feeling as if we have accomplished our goal. Little did I know this final journey would be so difficult. I seriously believed this fourth pilgrimage would be the easy one!

Tom and I began our relationship as amateur hikers and campers. In our early marriage years, we spent summers high in the Pecos

Wilderness of the Sangre de Cristo Mountains of New Mexico, tramping the trails, rock climbing, and staring as sunsets spilled their tinted red blaze over the mountain peaks. We gingerly crossed swiftly flowing creeks, usually balancing on wobbly logs thrown across the water, laughing when one of us fell in. We loved to stalk forest creatures for just a glimpse of them, the occasional porcupine or bear. But my favorite wildlife "catch" was a stellar jay making his grating call while flashing a blue wing as he moved from tree to tree. Each summer, these forays into the New Mexico mountains became our plan of escape from our institutional world in Oklahoma where we lived and worked.

Our most treasured hike took us to a little hidden meadow a couple of miles off the Windsor Trail out of the Santa Fe Ski Basin. This was our Shangri-La, our mountain paradise. Hauling in heavy backpacks we groaned up the steep mountain trails, through the aspen forests, across two running creeks with a final assault up a steep slope. But regardless of the strain, each summer we excitedly threw those matching red packs onto our backs and hauled our sweaty selves to the rim of the meadow, usually arriving about mid-afternoon.

Discovered by only a miniscule number of hikers for the almost forty years we trekked into that lovely space, delight filled our hearts as we crested the small rise that gave us our first glimpse into the valley below. Upon arrival, we shared our elation with a hug, bumping our bulky backpacks against each other. The hike into this pristine meadow (which we named Arrowhead Meadow because of its shape) was not an easy one. Only seasoned hikers tried this one!

After pitching our well-used tent under the shade of massive Ponderosa pines, we would nestle like squatters for a week or so, sharing the forested spaces with deer, bear, coyotes, and ranging cows. These times became the pinnacle of our precious days together as a married couple.

Then our children grew older and our careers developed into work with more demanding obligations. Our romantic summer jaunts lessened as we found our schedule would allow us to backpack into Arrowhead Meadow only once or twice a summer. Those trips became invaluable to our psyches, deepening our connection with the mountains and each other.

In the next stage of life, our children left home. We bought a summer place in a little ski village in the northern mountains of New Mexico that kept us attached and closer to civilization. We began to hike and camp in Arrowhead Meadow less often, maybe every other year or so. I began to feel incomplete somehow, having not seen the sunlight splash across the meadow or the tiny stream that flowed through it. A chasm of painful separation formed in my heart as we lost contact with this sacred space.

Then life sped by in a blaze of years. We woke up one day and somehow we had aged. We no longer backpacked into Arrowhead Meadow. At age eighty-plus, Tom could no longer carry a heavy backpack and hike due to an imbalance issue he had developed. So for a few years we simply hiked up once during the summers wearing much smaller daypacks. Those days in the heights continued to inspire us, but then the inevitable coming of the dusk forced us to hike out of the mountains and return to our car. The drive back down into Santa Fe was invariably quiet, while each of us reminisced in our minds about the day.

As I write down these words, Tom and I have not been into the meadow for more than two years. Tom is less able now to make even the day hike. The trail is rough and rocky, which causes him to stumble. I find I do not want to go without him because that space was *ours* for such a long time. Adapting to our age differences and to aging itself brings with it pain, loss and sadness. One of my motives for creating the pilgrimages for myself is precisely to face this reality in my life. I do not want to live in depression and sadness as I continually surrender activities and connections in my waning days. Surely there is another way to age!

This fourth pilgrimage reveals my last attempt to recover our earlier days of hiking like free spirits upon the lands we love. Little did I know that this journey would turn into another broken vow. This last pilgrimage during my seventieth birthday year becomes another essential lesson to my project of intentional aging.

My first three pilgrimages, I must admit, were astonishing journeys of growth, satisfaction, change and courage. I felt invincible when I returned to Santa Fe after those treks. But the Vermont pilgrimage became a metaphor for the realities of aging and life, sobering my delight and sense of accomplishment from the first three. So this pilgrimage brings us full circle to chapter 1 of this book, except I am different now. In this pilgrimage, I must face many of the vicissitudes of aging, in both Tom and me. But because the first three pilgrimages affected me so profoundly, I find it necessary to cope with the Vermont experiences differently than I might have in the past. My consciousness has evolved. Yet the lessons of life continue, and not all of them are comfortable to the soul.

With the reality of Tom's age and limitations plaguing me, I make my plans for the pilgrimage to Vermont, trusting that he will be able to hike the trails. I research the maps as best I could and ask the guide to place us on easier trails so that my spouse could make the hikes each day without too much difficulty. Tom is eighty-three as the pilgrimage is planned. While he is still strong and a good walker, he does have difficulty navigating roots and rocks. I naively had no idea that the trails in Vermont were nothing but roots and rocks, as we learned on our first day out.

For our beginning hike we are dropped off by our guide, Bruce, to walk the Beane Trail, which peels off the Long Trail and heads straight up a steep pathway to a shelter known as the Birch Glen Camp. However, we first missed the turn onto the Beane and walked about two miles out of the way before running into another hiker who steered us back to our intended path. Time is lost and meanwhile, the sky fills with clouds; rain is imminent. Deep ruts quickly begin to give Tom trouble with his footing. Instead of enjoying the beauty of the surroundings, I grow anxious and worried for the safety of my spouse. He has fallen on much easier trails than this one. Tension rises in my spine as I watch him stumble up the trail. I stop and stare at the trail ahead, feeling a bit guilty. Have I made a mistake asking Tom to join me on this fourth pilgrimage? I wonder.

After another hour or so passes, with neither of us speaking very often while we slowly climb the intimidating trail, we arrive at the shelter. The clouds are low and heavy as mist begins to fall on our hats and shoulders. Locating a place underneath the shelter to stop and discuss our situation, we don our rain gear. Raindrops softly ding on the tin roof warning us they will soon grow in intensity. We have no idea how far it is to the end of the trail where the guide is supposed to retrieve us. What we do know is that we have spent far too much time trying to find the shelter. A quandary presents itself: Do we go back down the mountain or continue the steady climb upward? Finally, with a complete lack of confidence in our decision, we resolve to continue. What urges us on is embarrassment. How could we have become lost and then mired in this demanding trail so early in our trip—our first day out?

I suppose the universe begins to feel sorry for us at this point because another hiker appears before us on the trail. He is tall and lean, with appropriate gear, which signals to us that he is a serious hiker. With the typical brevity of a Vermont resident, the stranger answers our questions about the trail to our destination point and then moves on with a long stride that covers turf quickly, causing him to disappear in seconds. Tom and I glance at each other, regroup and return to our unsteady upward plodding.

To our surprise about a half hour later, the veteran hiker returns, heading straight for us. After quickly introducing himself, Bill seems intent on talking to us, stating flatly that he is a "search and rescue" first responder. Stupidly we did not make the connection. He tries again, a bit more bluntly to clue us to his purpose. Knowing we will be unable to make it to the end of our designated hike before dark, he queries in staccato fashion, "Do you have flashlights? Do you have a proper map? Do you know where you are going? Are you aware there are bears in these forests?"

Bill asks these questions in rapid-fire succession while making it crystal clear that he does not want to be back in the woods after dark searching for us. His tone tells me that he is obviously convinced this is precisely what will happen if we keep walking. I mumble that we realize the situation is not safe. We reluctantly make a promise to return to the beginning of the trail. Once again Bill strides away, just as quickly as the first time we saw him.

I try my phone to apprise Bruce of our return to him so he will know to wait for us. No service, of course! So far not much seems to be going well for us! Despondently we turn ourselves around and head back down the trail, a heavy sense of failure resting on both our shoulders, not sure at all that Bruce will be waiting for us since this had not been our agreement.

Our first day out, and we could not even complete the first hike. This portends a really long, disappointing pilgrimage! As we leave the trail and come to the paved road, we see Bruce lounging beside his car. He looks up as he hears us crunching our way through the leaves, surprised that we have returned to rejoin him. It is his fortune and ours that he has not driven to the negotiated point. I can tell on his face that he is now wondering who has hired him and how much trouble we are going to be for the week. Bruce seems annoyed. An awkward silence pervades the car as he drives us to the first of our guest inns.

Forty-eight hours later this story almost repeats itself. Our intrepid tour guide drops us for a nine-mile hike at a trailhead leading deep into the Moosalamoo National Recreation area. Bruce is confident we will arrive in great shape at the Blueberry Hill Inn located close to Goshen, with exciting tales about the forest covered in ravishing autumn colors. No mention is made of our previous false start. All three of us are in good spirits as we are deposited at the trailhead. Little does Bruce know that if Tom and I can disagree on directions and trails, we will. Both of us are firstborns with independent take-charge, competent, competitive personalities. We seldom agree on how to accomplish a task; we just agree that the task must be done. Our Myers-Briggs letters are opposite; our Enneagram numbers don't match. Our childhood experiences are nothing alike, and our age difference gives us dissimilar worldviews. This information becomes important to understanding our dynamics as we begin this next hike.

Bruce drives away leaving us to our day. Our maps are spot on for the first fifty yards. Then a signpost appears loaded with unfamiliar symbols that don't match the map. The trail splits right here. Tom argues for taking one trail; I, of course, argue for the other. I am inwardly confident that I am right (of course), but as a wife keeping company with a husband who has a much keener sense of direction than I do, I cave to Tom's insistence that we should follow the trail to the left. We begin walking, and it soon becomes evident that this is not the right path.

Backtracking to the trailhead signpost, we start over, heading up the gentle slope in the direction I had originally suggested. Rather than feeling proud that I was correct about the trail I had argued for, I become concerned. Is this confusion another aging loss? Tom has always had such a sharp sense of direction and mapping capability. Suddenly I find myself wondering if this sensibility is failing him, leaving us both in danger of becoming quite disoriented and lost in these unfamiliar woods? Our map, hand drawn by our guide, provides me no comfort or confidence. For the rest of the day, I feel insecure and anxious about our hike. This feels nothing like my experience in the Cotswolds, where I was on strange trails with maps to figure out. Why was I confident there and uncomfortable here? What is happening?

Before long, Tom and I do settle into a rhythm for walking and begin to enjoy the fall foliage and the cool temperatures. The trail is wide because it is a cross-country ski trail, used by our guide in the winter. Just as I thought I might relax, we come to another signpost that does not match our map. A decision must be made. Once again we enter into an unpleasant debate about which way we should go. I am tired, thirsty, hungry, and discouraged. Tom is frustrated with the maps and poor signage. Just as we begin to seriously wonder what we should do, a woman comes bolting along the trail. As a runner, she seems to know where she is going. We ask for help, and she makes our decision for us. We go straight ahead rather than taking the trail to the right as the map seems to indicate.

This is our second difficult hiking day. Over and over again on this trek we find our maps and trail signposts to be inadequate. Only the kindness of other walkers rescues us from our fumbling decisions about which way to turn. Rather than the relaxing walks I had taken in the Cotswolds, so far these two days have been quite stressful.

Tom and I arrive at the Blueberry Hill Inn both mentally and physically exhausted. The only thing that saves the day is the stunning view across a pond perfectly situated behind the Inn. Fall weather has magnificently decorated the towering trees along the banks with oranges, reds, and yellows. Reflected in the calm water are the vivid colors seemingly plastered on a liquid canvas. "I don't think I have ever seen anything quite so beautiful!" I gasp. Tom nods. We grasp hands to silently acknowledge that though the day has been difficult, we are still in this together.

Heading straight for the Adirondack chairs scattered alongside the pond's edges, we collapse wearily, simply to sit and stare at the exquisite views before us. Resting in that peaceful space allows my mind to return to normal balance, as I tentatively remember a quote from *The Course of Love* by Alain de Botton, a book I had read to prepare for this pilgrimage:

"We don't need to be constantly reasonable in order to have good relationships; all we need to have mastered is the occasional capacity to acknowledge with good grace that we may, in one or two areas, be somewhat insane."

Some of the conflicts Tom and I had conjured throughout our day had been somewhat insane. Neither of us knew where we were on the trail, what we needed to be looking for, even where we were headed. Vermont is not our familiar terrain. We had a hand-drawn map and a trail under our feet. That is all that was available to guide us because the signposts in the Vermont forests resemble nothing we are familiar with in the Rockies of New Mexico and Colorado. In addition, our worldviews on how to sort out the issues of our hiking dilemmas are quite different. I tend to anxiety; Tom tends to denial. These behaviors do not match!

At this point, the purpose of this fourth and final pilgrimage for me has not yet revealed itself.

As we enter the lovely Blueberry Inn, we both long for a hot shower, a good meal and a comfortable bed. All three wishes are granted. I fall into dreamless sleep that night, my body aching to recover so I can continue this strange, discomforting pilgrimage.

We rise the next day to hike out of the Inn to a lake not too far away, a beautiful picnic spot, easy to find. This day soothes our bruised egos and gives us a fresh sense of the Vermont trails. We decide to treat today as a day of rest, spending our time reading, talking, and enjoying the splendor of the golden autumn day. Okay, I can do this! I tell myself.

Our excitement and confidence is short-lived, however. For our next trek Bruce drives us to the point where we will begin a hike around Silver Lake, located amidst a group of trails wandering like spaghetti through the Moosalamoo Recreation area. We have a printed map this time, with Bruce's scribbling attached on a sticky note. A walk around a lake sounds serene and enjoyable, but we could not have been more wrong!

The hike starts out manageable enough. Bruce has coached us on how to follow the trail signs so we are better prepared at this point. However, before long we find ourselves faced with intimidating rocks that soon mutate into boulders, forcing us to climb around them to keep to the trail. I move ahead to scout out the easiest way through the boulder field. Glancing over my shoulder every few moments, I see Tom coming behind me, creeping and climbing his way through the sea of rocks. Every so often the trail provides us with a respite that fools us into thinking that maybe we are done with this boulder assault. But soon, these giants of stone are on our path again, and our ordeal resumes.

Time begins to crawl, just as we are crawling. Pulling ourselves along, we often have to drop down to the edge of the lake where there is no trail simply to move ourselves forward. We lose the trail signs from time to time and have to wander around through the boulder field, struggling to locate our path forward. There is no respite. The trail stretches haphazardly before us, up and over massive rocks, down again. I peer across the lake and see how far we have yet to go. What started out to be an easy stroll around a picturesque lake, at least in my mind, turns into a nightmare. I am worried sick about getting Tom through this mess without his breaking a leg. My sense of adventure turns into a sense of dread.

Fatigue sets in. We stop to rest. A group of younger hikers comes along, bouncing over the rocks like children on a playground, laughing and talking. Our age becomes evident in these encounters. After drinking from our water bottles and eating granola bars, we continue our project to circumnavigate this lake and survive. After what seems like endless hours of time, mountains and mountains of stones, scraped knees, banged-up shins, and several near falls, we do eventually escape the boulder field intact. Neither of us is too damaged from the hike.

A secluded picnic table at the top of a gentle hill in the trees entices us to keep moving, even though we are exhausted beyond belief. Finally, a break! Tom and I spread out our lunch and empty the last of our water from the plastic containers we have hauled around the lake on our backs. Too tired to talk, we munch slowly on our chicken salad sandwiches, wondering what in the world Bruce had been thinking when he said that we would "love this walk." Is he crazy? For me, this tortuous trip makes the English Lake District hikes with David Whyte seem quite moderate in comparison. I am not happy with this process! However, I do have presence of mind enough to dig my phone out of my hiking pants pocket and take shots of the lake with the sun bouncing across the ripples of water.

When Bruce gathered us up to take us on to our next bed and breakfast, we were speechless at his enthusiasm about the hike because he assumed we have enjoyed every minute of it. For a moment I found myself wondering if Bruce was some sort of madman to have suggested this hike for us!

In our quarters that evening at the Inn on Park Street in Brandon, I am pensive as Tom is taking his shower. Something shifted in me today on that grueling hike. Once when I turned around to check on Tom, I saw him struggling to make his body cooperate so he could accomplish the trek without falling. At that moment I became a caretaker in this marriage. Age wins! We *will* grow older. Our bodies *will* become limited. We must accept and adapt. My own lessons from the previous pilgrimages are now sharply in my face. There is no escape. Today's hike brings reality thundering home to me. This will be the last of this sort of hiking that Tom and I will do together as a married couple. Not that we won't continue to take hikes or walks, I surmise. But in the future I must be careful what I organize for him. It is unfair of me to refuse to face and accept our age-related differences.

The rest of the fourth pilgrimage passes without incident. Each day we are picked up at our bed and breakfast, carted off to a trailhead, given paper bags stuffed with a delicious homemade lunch complete with baked goodies, and handed a map to guide our way. The trees along each trail truly do catch my attention. The weather is next to perfect. One lightly cloudy, cool afternoon we stop at a maple sugar farm to witness the processing of Vermont maple syrup. I could not resist buying some of the tasty, dark liquid to ship back home. Having never actually seen maple-syrup-making before, I am fascinated by all of the lines running through the trees and the equipment in the wooden buildings. Right there on the spot, I fall in love with Vermont!

One particularly humorous experience occurs during this pilgrimage to counter the more difficult tales of the trip. As happens upon long walks for seniors, the body has the urge to make a "stop in the woods for nature's call." However, one day our map takes us off the forested trail onto a paved road with cabins occasionally scattered throughout the woods along the way. The land is now no longer public forestland; it is private land. This setting does not seem right for a "pit stop" for either of us. Tom is beginning to feel the urge strongly enough that I am aware something better change quickly. I speed up, walking ahead of him, peering into the trees and bushes to find a place for him to stop. Looking to my right and left, nothing looks appropriate.

Walking faster than usual, I round a bend in the road and then stop dead still. I burst out laughing! Tom gains speed and catches up to me to see why I am carrying on like this. Then we both start giggling as he spots it too: a bright blue port-a-potty—right there in the edge of the woods, about thirty yards off the road! Running for the plastic door, Tom grins and disappears inside. I take photos of the "toilet in the woods" and post them online as our accomplishment of the day. What a delightful gift right here in the middle of the woods of Vermont, with little else around to explain why this toilet would be on this backcountry road! Nothing aids seniors like the appropriately placed option for relieving the bladder! As we walk away giggling, I turn around to see if the little blue closet is still there. I am almost convinced that this much-appreciated convenience is pure magic and will somehow vanish as we leave the scene. It doesn't.

Another afternoon our guide takes us to a graveyard with headstones dating back to the 1800s and little flags staked in the ground throughout the area. These afternoon drives we take through the winding roads lined with vivid autumn colors make me feel that I have stepped onto a movie set. Every turn in the road only casts a more gorgeous view upon the horizon. Our final hike is along a river with an overlook of the Champlain Valley. We descend into the valley to walk along the river's edges. I am mesmerized by the leaves, as they float through the air like feathers, landing on the ground to provide a crunchy carpet for us. Every fall color imaginable is present in vivid splendor. Unable to help myself, I begin picking up various particularly fetching leaves and stuffing them in my pockets. As soon as my pockets are full, I locate a wonderfully smooth boulder about the size of a small footstool resting in a tiny cove of shallow water. I bend over to spread the leaves across the surface of the rock, like an artist creating a painting.

The portrait of leaves becomes a symbol of this fourth pilgrimage for me. The leaves are dazzling right now, but they will fade and die. The rocks will remain long after the leaves have floated off down the river and turned to compost. This metaphor is not lost on me as I meander downstream with Tom in front of me. We are the leaves, in the autumn of our lives turning to winter. Our color is fading; our energy is almost spent; our time of productivity will soon be past. And the cycle continues… interestingly, there is something comforting in this reality that life continues, even if I won't be here to experience it.

The highlight of this pilgrimage comes close to the end of the trip. Our guide takes us to the village of Ripton, where we visit the unpainted, wooden summer home of Robert Frost. Both Tom and I are lovers of this man's poetry, so this venture is one of our most meaningful stories of the pilgrimage. Wandering around the cleared grounds, we peer into the house through the opaque windows. Squinting through the screens, we can barely see his kitchen and living room, sparsely furnished and rustic. A screened porch off the back of the house hints that the poet might have sat outside on dusky evenings listening to untamed creatures as they rustled through the foliage on their nocturnal forages. In front of the cabin sits a stone bench. Tom and I plop down on it to reflect on the man and his life, sharing the meager stories we know about Robert Frost. I sigh, breathing in the crisp, damp air. Life just does not get much better than this!

Bruce now drives us to the Robert Frost Interpretative Trail, where we walk for a couple of hours over maintained paths and bridges into the thick trees where Frost often hiked. The trail is lined with huge metal panels etched with his poetry. *The Road Not Taken* is the favorite for most people, judging by the ruts in the path in front of the panel. I take a photo of this one to keep with me as a reminder of the day. Most of us do choose the more common path in life, especially as we retire. In fact, most of us are fairly predictable throughout our lives. But on this pilgrimage Frost's poetry is a stark reminder that to practice intentional aging requires us to take the path less traveled because we must become conscious and aware of our choices, decisions, and intentions in order to enter into the Wisdom Years.

The fourth pilgrimage of my seventieth year comes to an end with our sitting on the Adirondack line train as it races toward New York City's Penn Station. My heart beats with a bit of grief that my four birthday pilgrimages are now completed. Whatever is going to happen has happened with these ventures into my own aging project. Yet something in me knows that there is so much yet ahead. These pilgrimages will require reflection, interpretation and application to my life. The "road" I travel now will make all the difference in my life. Of this, I am sure.

CHAPTER 9:
AND REALITY

PILGRIMAGE 4:
THE INTERIOR JOURNEY

We learn, too, that being another's servant is not humiliating—
quite the opposite, for it sets us free from the wearying
responsibility of continuously catering to our own twisted,
insatiable natures. We learn the relief and privilege of being
granted something more important to live for than ourselves.
—Alain de Botton

Actor Matthew McConaughey confesses that he likes to create adages for himself. Doing this reminds him to stay authentic in a profession that can easily be experienced as somewhat artificial. Recently on a late-night talk show, McConaughey revealed his most recent axiom, "I found myself right where I left me!" Could any truer words be spoken for all of us?

Just about the time we come to feel competent or confident about ourselves, the universe reminds us that we are still who we are, warts and all, and a bit of humility is not a bad thing to cultivate. After three meaningful pilgrimages designed to discover an inner resource for cultivating my Wisdom Years, I come to Vermont only to "find myself right where I left me." The insights to which I have given birth through these journeys of soul do reside deeply within. I know what my inner work must be. Some of it I have already begun to execute with good results for developing my way through to the

Wisdom Years. Because most of us are unable to repair and transform ourselves very quickly, I bring "myself" to Vermont, personal issues and all. The hike through the boulder field around Silver Lake teaches me this unpleasant truth: A few breakthroughs in my behaviors and thinking do not a complete transformation make. I still have so much interior work to do.

When was your last "uh, oh, here I am, being myself" moment?

Thus the reality of this fourth pilgrimage dawns on me with painful awareness. The walking and hiking experiences remind me that my previous pilgrimages took place in another space and time. They were sacred trips with astonishing outcomes in terms of my own personal growth. But no one lives merely by themselves, walking around in the Cotswolds or hiking the deserts of Arizona on a daily basis. Actual life takes place in our homes and relationships, communities, and neighborhoods. The insights I gained must be applied to daily living for the purpose of my soul journey to be authentic.

The Vermont pilgrimage demonstrates unequivocally what seniors will truly face and negotiate as we age, or else what I have actually done is to complete three rather unusual vacations. I do not want this untruth to become my story. These pilgrimages are a sincere attempt to awaken my psyche to the realities of aging, both positive and negative. I long to create in my mind and heart a deliberate sense of meaning and purpose that will guide the remainder of my life. I wholeheartedly desire to become conscious of the arduous path ahead in a way that I might live out my days with gratitude and fortitude. Isn't this what most of us desire?

From the very first day, the Vermont pilgrimage does not resemble the previous trips. This pilgrimage turns out to be my much-needed life transformation rather than a series of insights for me to ponder and accept. Here I am on the cusp of the Wisdom Years. I can feel it now. While tears of regret and hope simultaneously appear in my eyes, I feel the certainty of this reality in this present moment. Climbing through the massive, demanding boulders around Silver Lake, I surrender. Here, right here among these bold and beautiful rocks emerges the painful truth: I have now become a caretaker for my spouse. I must stop wrestling with the inevitability of my aging process and adapt and change!

All the issues that hound us as we age stare directly in my face. Don't get me wrong! Tom does a magnificent job of climbing through the rugged terrain with me. His usual jovial self is evident as we clamber through the boulder field. But I see how he has to struggle as he climbs, how slow and deliberate he has to be, how intensely he must concentrate. His age is a definite reality; my reality is just moments behind. Right now, our lived situation demands that I assume the role as his caretaker. Who knows when the roles could reverse, and then he would be required to care for me? For this is the truth of the matter. One of us will likely care for the other for the rest of our lives. And when one of us is gone, the remaining partner becomes his or her own caretaker, or perhaps a child or grandchild has to step in and perform the job.

Because all Elderlies are not married or have children or grandchildren, it becomes imperative at this point for me to mention that aging as a truly single person creates its own set of issues. I know more than a handful of seniors who have come into their aging years without any immediate family to be their support system. By the way, this is not a rare situation. Several single retirees whom I know personally are diligently and intentionally building a network of friendships to help carry them through the final years of their lives. In some cases this is an excellent strategy for aging as a single. In other circumstances, this approach does not net the senior the desired results.

While being a single senior who does not have immediate family to assist could produce loneliness and despair, this does not necessarily have to be the way things are. Today's Baby Boomers are rapidly creating retirement settings all around the country for singles, including retirement villages. Graded living situations are growing like weeds in most towns of any size so that singles can move from independent living, to assisted living, to nursing care, to death. The available opportunities and activities in these settings usually include numerous ways to create connections and friendships. Religious institutions are also quite adept these days at attending to the social needs of senior adults simply because so many congregations are gray-haired. Most towns and cities have senior centers where net-works can be formed. Many universities offer senior educational and travel programs allowing seniors to nurture new friendships. There is no lack of possibilities for connection within the senior years.

The real issue for senior singles becomes, however, those final years or days of life when one truly needs assistance. Who will be there for those for whom this is a reality? Who will come to visit in nursing homes or hospice? Who will care for these seniors in the final years of life or help attend the final death arrangements? The only response possible is, of course, friends, neighbors, distant relatives or hired caretakers. Seniors in this situation may also find themselves being forced to move in order to find appropriate care. This reality makes facing these issues as single Elderlies one of crit-ical importance. It might be worth seeking advice or counseling from someone in a senior services organization to help sort through all the issues that arise when we meet our final years truly alone and without much support.

The saddest story I know concerns a woman whose care needs have worn out all her friendships, creating a situation of isolation and desperation in her final years. She needs more care just as there are fewer people to help. There is a danger in placing demands on friends that should belong to professional caretakers, such as bathing, grooming, providing meals. Single seniors without imme-diate family might do well to remember that close friends, though usually helpful and generous, are not family members. What can be asked of friends or neighbors is not the same as what might be asked of family members.

The most joyful situation I have heard was a news story about a single, elderly woman who lived alone, depressed and desperate to have people in her life. A younger neighbor noticed that the older woman had no visitors or caretakers. So the neighbor stepped in and drew this woman into her family and care circle. Immediately this aging senior found an intergenerational community, including children, which gave her a new lease on life. This fortune, in turn, improved the senior's health and her spirits, most likely giving her a few extra years to live. This story proves to be a far better model for the burgeoning aging population that is filling our neighborhoods. Perhaps if our local communities began to create networks of inter-generational "families," so many single seniors would find love and compassion in their final years, rather than dying alone and lonely.

Spreading before us, the boulder field is daunting, like an undesirable assignment. Then without warning in my psyche, the unforgiving rocks transform from a rugged hike into a metaphor for aging. With no sympathy the massive stones demand unrelenting attention and discipline. My brain is on high alert! I must protect Tom and guide him through the field as best I can. And if a problem occurs, I will be the one who finds the way to rescue us.

As I sit here writing these words a year later, the Vermont pilgrimage has become our lived reality. Tom is ill at the moment. The situation may or may not be serious. We do not yet know. But the very fact that I have spent the week caring for him has planted the seeds of understanding in my mind and heart: This is what aging truly looks like! So what good have my pilgrimages been in the face of actual illness, caretaking, concern, fear, suffering, anxiety? Did I really learn anything that will help me confront what the senior years can fling at us? I believe I did. Let's review.

The first pilgrimage into the Superstition Mountains of Arizona reminds me that as I age, strength and stamina become even more necessary. Our bodies weaken. Our abilities are more and more limited. In a split second, we can easily become frail and fragile. Thus daily nurturing of our body becomes vital to aging well. Every bite we eat, every step we take, every night's rest we get, every book we read becomes not only what we enjoy, but also the activities that enhance our health and well-being. This process includes awakening and attending to our mental and spiritual capacities as well. If I am going to become a caretaker, then it does matter how I take care of myself so that I may do the job as needed.

The first pilgrimage adventure in the Chaco Canyon of New Mexico taught me that courage is necessary as we age. To challenge my fear of heights, I had to face myself and climb that wall, fears and all. To become a caretaker means facing one of our greatest fears—that we will lose our loved ones. This week my mind has been awash with a myriad of emotions. Is this my new reality? Am I watching the beginning of my beloved's full decline? Am I up to the task for what all of this means for both of us? Is Tom afraid? Is he having confusing or clarifying thoughts about aging and dying? It is time to talk about the hard stuff!

We attended the funeral of an extended family member last weekend. As we both sat in a room packed with people over eighty, I glanced at the flag-draped casket surrounded by flowers and thought, "Most of the people in this room will not be alive in ten years. Will Tom or I be in that group?" "How many years before my family and friends attend my memorial service?" For some reason, these thoughts were not depressing, but they did vividly etch themselves into my mind. Funerals and memorial services will now become a part of my ordinary life whether I like it or not.

A friend and I found ourselves joking about this stage of life when we feel we should purchase a "funeral outfit" because we will have need of this attire more and more as we age. And then today, only four days after the family funeral, a letter arrives from another grieving spouse telling us his wife, our friend Sally, has recently died. Both Tom and I are inundated with memories of our time with this couple. We write a sympathy card to send to George, hoping our words are not too trite. What does one say in times like this? Words do not seem enough. The ritual of dying and death no longer occupies the corners of faraway universes for those of us in our senior years. Dying and death are now up close and personal! It's time to face this reality squarely and with courage.

One of the best articles I have read on facing and accepting death, including our own was written by Judy Lief, a Buddhist teacher, and author of *Making Friends with Death*. Her insight about death is that this undeniable reality is our best teacher, and lives with us every moment since we have been born. She states, "Death turns out to be the teacher who releases us from fear. It's the teacher that opens our hearts to a more free-flowing love and appreciation for life and one another."

Then there is the other reality—that we might be the ones who need care. To place ourselves in the hands of a caretaker means we may be in our most fragile if not final days. In order to do this well, we must claim the courage that so often eludes us: the courage to face our vulnerabilities. Most of us are uncomfortable with the need to ask others to help us. When we are young, we cannot imagine being so frail that we are unable to fulfill basic human needs. We cannot imagine our dignity so compromised that we are reduced to being an infant again. But this is coming for most seniors at some point. Our most concentrated effort to be courageous will be called upon to face these inevitabilities.

Our Wisdom Years, as I discovered on my third pilgrimage in the Cotswolds, will demand of us that we live without a desire to be recognized as someone important. To put this into psycho-spiritual language: Living with intention encourages us to manifest humility as one of our guiding principles. Caretaking insists that we put the other person first. Their needs override our own for much of the time we are with them. In order to do this with gratitude and grace, we have to surrender attachment to our own egos on behalf of the needs of the other. Compassion becomes the requisite necessity in such times.

When I stood in that wheat field in the Cotswolds and realized that I was anonymous, even for those brief moments, that all my titles did not matter in the grand scheme of things, this insight began to guide me into the Wisdom Years. Today my titles and accomplishments do not matter as my spouse calls on me to do a simple task for him. I cannot say, "I was a university administrator and faculty member, so I should not have to get you a glass of water." Those words do not function in these settings, do they? (Or any other, for that matter!) Only compassion and humility are appropriate when we are caretaking for someone we love. The freedom I felt standing in that field in the Cotswolds has to be applied in this situation with Tom. The questions arise: Do I feel trapped in having to take care of him? Or do I instead feel the freedom and privilege of being able to be his caretaker? Do I resent having to bring him his pills and food? Or do I feel joy and freedom at being able to serve this beloved mate of mine?

Our attitudes toward these realities of aging are choices we make. I am choosing, even as I write these words, how to respond to my situation. While we are unable to choose the length of our days or the frailties that will befall us, we can determine the attitude we bring to the task of aging. The quality of this journey into our senior years is determined solely by our ability to adapt to and accept what comes to our door and find purpose in it. We can choose to dance the dance or sit on the sidelines and grumble.

This fourth pilgrimage teaches me a most valuable lesson from all the pilgrimages I walked this year: to live with awareness and presence on behalf of the other. Inside this insight resides the "doing" of the senior years. Our ability to act on behalf of others without need for recognition and approval becomes our deepest call to service in life. This life becomes, as we age, pure gift, nothing more, nothing less.

As this book is completed, we learn that my spouse is coping with a chronic issue like many of us, and he will have to adjust to living with changes in his body. What arose from this experience, both Tom and I confess, is that the future reality of caretaking for at least one of us is closer than we dare to imagine. This practice run taught us some valuable, if not painful lessons. First, we learned something ordinary and basic: that having the right equipment around the home for bathing, feeding, transporting and aiding the other is a must. Throughout each day as I helped with Tom's daily functions, I realized that to be cared for required proper equipment in order for him to be mobile. This is why so many seniors have handicapped paraphernalia scattered throughout the house. An awareness of the presence of illness becomes manifest in canes, walkers, wheel chairs, guard rails, bathtub stools, blankets tossed onto chairs and beds, medical supplies scattered on the counters. As I glanced at our home one day I noticed how our usually neat house was suddenly covered with items that served as a constant reminder that Tom was ill. This had become our new normal. Once again, adapt and change!

Secondly, I learned that our usual patterns of life together unexpectedly changed. Things like sleeping side by side, which we have done for so many years, taking our morning walks, sharing chores and tasks around the home, running errands together. All of this changed for the three weeks he was intensely ill and virtually immobile. As we age together, this is a foretaste of things to come, a sudden and jarring reality check. The pressure on couples is particularly painful because illness and infirmity can cause the couple to come apart in so many ways. The relationship changes are deceptively slow, moving from lovers and friends, to parent and child. All of this can be done with intention and with love, but to do so requires intense mindfulness and a willingness to adapt. A bit of humor thrown in for good measure is not a bad thing either! Tom and I found ourselves giggling over several silly incidents as we adjusted to our new situation.

The interior reality of Tom's illness for me was a shock of loneliness. Tom and I spend so much of our daily living in proximity to each other. We are a joined-at-the-hip type of couple. We like each other's company; our values are similar; we enjoy most activities together. To abruptly find myself forced into separation from him by this illness was unnerving and disruptive to my understanding of our "coupleness," and myself as a life partner. So many partners express these same feelings as age takes its toll on our relationships. As I stated in chapter 1, the truth of longevity comes with a price that is not necessarily pleasant to accept. To plow through all the situations ahead for those of us who will experience longevity requires us to be fully present and prepared in a way no other stage of life demands.

Most difficult for both of us was our emotional well-being. Tom found himself frustrated that he was rather suddenly limited in motion, forced to sit or lie down for days on end. This reality made him rather grumpy and argumentative. These emotions are not unusual for someone who has been active his entire life and is abruptly shut down. Likewise, I found myself frustrated and even frightened as I watched Tom's normally pleasant and positive personality change right before my eyes. Illness does this to most people, creates a change in our personality until we accept the illness and move on through it. (The film *Stronger*, starring Jake Gyllenhaal, demonstrates the truth of this situation.)

Though Tom and I managed to move through the worst of this medical situation, the lessons it offered both of us were startling, to say the least. We both were not at our best on some occasions as the days wore on in a stream of suffering and frustration. What a synchronicity that as I am writing this book, I am also living with the reality that I wish to express: The Wisdom Years do not come to us easily or without intentional awareness. The insights and under-standing fostered by my pilgrimage year reveal to me the heart of the matter for seniors seeking to engage their Wisdom Years: Courage, Presence, Compassion, and Service, the age-old lessons. Now I get it!

CHAPTER 10:
THE WISDOM YEARS

Our lives happen in between the deeds and ideas
that define us. Each of us feels it, the mystery, the
strangeness of life on earth. Of life and death.
—Simon Fitzmaurice

Life is available only in the present moment.
—Thich Nhat Hanh

Wisdom is not a given. Just because as seniors we have reached an age to claim our Social Security, retire from our careers, sport gray hair and wrinkles, and take the occasional cruise does not guarantee that we have also developed the elusive virtue of wisdom. There are far too many unwise senior adults, making plenty of unwise decisions and choices, living without the depth of consciousness necessary to explore intentionally the aging years. Wisdom is not a numbers game. It does not arrive on our doorstep like an Amazon package, forty-eight hours after an order has been placed to make one wise. Nor is the path like the yellow brick road that ends up at the Wizard's massive wooden door.

No. Wisdom comes slowly, silently, forged with effort and commitment. In fact, we often do not recognize when it is appropriate to claim that we are wise persons. The ego so cleverly fools us into thinking we have become a sage, when in reality we have far to go before we can legitimately attain this status. I find that those who bodaciously claim to be wise create in me an urge to run away. So before I dare to write a chapter on wisdom, allow me to be the first to say that I am unsure whether my pilgrimage year produced any measurable amount of elder wisdom inside my heart, mind, and actions. Only those who live around me could speak to the matter. What I can say is this: I know much more about what wisdom requires of seniors than I did before I walked those four journeys. I do know this process of becoming a wise soul will not be easy. What will be required of me, and you, too, if you are so inclined, is deliberate determination to create a life of courage and compassion that makes even a slight shift toward living into the Wisdom Years. Wisdom has as much to do with our will and intention as it does with our actual age and accumulated life experiences. Thus, I begin with a story:

His name was Bob. He is long gone now. But the imprint he left on my heart and soul are indelible. When I met him, Bob was already a senior adult, in his mid-seventies. One bright Sunday morning this man magically appeared in the church narthex where I served as pastor in Aurora, Colorado. A congenial smile and twinkling blue eyes framed his wrinkled face. Bob possessed a shock of thinning white hair that refused to hide his hearing aids. I thoroughly appreciated this impeccably dressed elf and his "old school" attire. On Sunday mornings when no one else wore one, Bob arrived in a well-cut suit, his shoes buffed to a shine, a perfectly knotted tie that matched his jacket and the flawless coordinating kerchief peeking out of his front pocket. A huge cloud of warmth completely surrounded his slender build and short stature, which caused children frequently to dash up and hug him around the knees.

Bob made himself at home in the midst of this small church family, quickly forming friendships and easily becoming the church mascot. His infectious smile was topped by only one thing: He was also our "love angel." Bob hugged everyone from the smallest child to the eldest member with a hold so hard and long that it took your breath away. And if you were a person uncomfortable with hugs, it was just too bad for you because Bob would not be put off. He turned that irresistible, warm light-beam onto everyone in his path. Even the most stoically rigid person was enticed into Bob's hugs and hearty handshakes. Looking squarely into our eyes, with his hands holding our shoulders, he boldly stated to each and every person, "I love you."

As the self-designated greeter, Bob stood at the front doors greeting everyone who walked in, member and stranger alike. His powerful message soon took over the ethos of the church family, and our congregation morphed into a lively, joyful group of people. No one seemed to understand who or what caused the shift, but I did. And I continually found myself thanking Bob for bringing his light, his love, and his presence through those church doors every week.

This man lived as one of the wisest persons I have ever known. Bob did not possess a plethora of college degrees; his career had been spent as a machinist. He had no wealth or special titles in any of the ways society deems valuable. He was not a public speaker, or a singer, or an athlete. Bob simply loved people, and he expected us to be a loving congregation with each other. With simple language his message spread: "Love one another as you have been loved." He was not gifted with words to overwhelm or enthrall an audience. His comments were usually plain spoken. Bob *was* his message. His feelings matched his actions, his simple words and his presence among us. I witnessed on more than one occasion his power to negotiate through the sometimes difficult or testy politics that would arise from time to time among the congregants. He cut no quarter for those who wanted to fight simply to be disagreeable. Though he was generally gentle in demeanor, he was not afraid of tough talk if this is what was needed. For Bob, love solved all problems.

This authentic and wise man made all the difference in the tone of our congregation. When I asked visitors later what caused them to join with our church, most responded with a smile and said, "There's this really cheerful man at the front door giving out hugs as you come in!" I would chuckle to myself, "That Bob! How does he do it?"

Although I knew Bob years ago in my fifties, I became aware even then that I stood in the presence of an unusual human being. When my ideas about wisdom were still undeveloped, I found myself watching, listening, learning from this master teacher whose very life taught me the lessons I have needed as I age. I fully understood at the time that I had a long way to go before I could join him, if I ever could.

What I wish to develop for myself after these four pilgrimages is a life principle of sorts: *To manifest Wisdom within that evolves into*

Presence without. To be intentional about aging requires that we be aware of and attentive to the myriad experiences created by our emotions, thoughts, actions, desires, imaginings. In turn, our intentions then are able to transform into the principle or virtue of wisdom. The expression "Wisdom is Presence" reveals our ability to "be here now" as we live out our senior years. It's not just what we experience that forms wisdom; it's also what we put out into the world. Are we fully here and available to others? Do we offer our Presence—our full attention and compassion—to the world as gift and grace?

Perhaps the best tack to take at this juncture would be to define how I am using the word *presence.* On the one hand I could be misconstrued simply to mean "to be here in body, present and accounted for." Most of us spend much of life in this mode. Can you remember the last time you were simply a body in a room, rather than a Presence in that same room? Most of us can easily conjure such an image about ourselves. For me, I imagine myself sitting in a dentist's waiting room only to find I am just a body filling a faux leather chair. But authentic *presence of self* demands much more of us than to simply be here as an occupant of space.

For a decade beginning in my thirties I carried with me at all times a copy of a tiny book titled, *The Practice of the Presence of God* by Brother Lawrence, a seventeenth-century Carmelite monk. I read it through most days or weeks, working to ingest the words that would guide me toward my own spiritual destiny forty years later. I have long outgrown most of the ancient piety contained in this little gem of a book, but the concept of Presence has stayed with me. Bob "practiced presence" with everyone he met. His wisdom was evident in how he negotiated life, as one whose natural tendency was love and compassion, strength and courage, kindness and generosity, regardless of the situation. He served others simply by accepting them as they came to him. His Presence challenged each of us to be open, available, kind, and helpful to everyone around us.

The most useful tool I have found for explaining and integrating the concept of Presence for myself at this stage of life derives from my experience with Mindfulness training. Remember when I mentioned this in an earlier chapter? My brief encounter with Mindfulness

Meditation teacher John Bruna taught me the importance of living with Presence. His explanation urged awareness of what is going on around us in as many of our waking moments as possible. While I am sitting here at my desk writing, I am to be cognizant, "Do I feel the air from my back door blowing against my skin? Am I able to hear the car passing by outside my window, and the voices of the children laughing in the alleyway behind my house? Do I feel the seat of the chair on which I am sitting as I write these words? Am I aware of my feet as they rest against the wooden floor, or my fingers as they fly over the computer keyboard? Do I sense my breath, in and out, in and out? Are there smells in the air that invade my nostrils?" Being mindful of the environment where we are located for this particular moment in time helps set the stage for living in the moment. Being aware of our setting and our place right now starts a deeper process within our minds. And this is only the beginning.

For years as a pastor, I led workshops and retreats on prayer as the central tool which nurtures a life of spiritual depth. I still believe this. However, at this stage of life—as an Elderly—I have come to understand that the other side of the coin is the ability to also *listen,* which is encompassed in meditation and mindfulness. The practice of prayer invites us to voice ourselves to the Divine; mindfulness calls us to listen to the Presence of the Divine with us and within us. It is this balance of speaking *and* listening to the deeper Presence that shapes the spiritual life belonging to Wisdom. This is not a new idea, by any means, but one that so often has to be repeated in order for us to remember to practice this discipline.

Bob was quite aware that Presence constitutes what humans really crave from one another. We naturally desire full attention from another, not their assessment or judgment of us, or their partial ear. From the other we solicit their care for us, their respect for our humanity, compassion for our suffering. We crave to be heard, loved, cherished with attention and affection. We yearn for genuine Presence from our fellow humans so that we might feel that our being here on Earth matters. One of the greatest fabrications sold to Americans is that we can be so fully independent that we don't need anyone else. This is simply untrue! Human beings are relational creatures. This certainty guides most of our actions and interactions.

This truth of connection is easily witnessed when we are with children. If a child does not receive appropriate attention, then they will seek a response by acting inappropriately or misbehaving. Children do this because usually they have an inherent need to be acknowledged. It matters that they matter! Adults are no different. Especially as we age, seniors struggle with how to feel included and accepted because the usual means are now mostly completed: careers, parenting, and for some, marriages. Just as life tends to reduce our connections, sincere attention from others becomes key to our well-being the older we become. The desire to bond and stay connected becomes even more critical to the quality of our days as Elderlies.

Yet entry into the path toward the Wisdom Years does not derive entirely from our own needs and desires, emotion, and thoughts. Wisdom itself blossoms when we offer ourselves willingly as Presence to the other, whether it be the grocery clerk, the UPS driver, a grandchild, our spouse, a neighbor, even a dog someone is walking. On a communal scale, we need to develop our Presence to be attentive to peoples who are strangers, to nations different from our own, to victims of tragedies like hurricanes and earthquakes, to the neighbor no one seems to visit. When we can transcend our miseries and our miniscule musings to turn our attention to the world around us and make ourselves truly present, we have planted the seeds for our Wisdom Years to flourish.

Bob made himself present simply by consistently giving himself to anyone who came into his space, openly, fully, with joy, and delight. He profoundly impacted others until the day he died, not because of wealth or education, status or titles, but because he intentionally lived among us with his authentic self, his full Presence. There was no hiddenness, narcissism, or covetousness in Bob. He was genuinely himself—humble, present, open, loving, compassionate. If I might, could I encourage you to rummage through your own list of friends and stories to discern who the "wise person" is or has been in your life? Why do you call this person wise? What qualities does he or she have that you should label them as a wise one? Do you desire these qualities in your own life? If so, to what purpose?

What my four pilgrimages most profoundly teach me to do is pay attention, to be present to the experiences of my life, and to yours. This includes both our exterior life and our interior world. In the Arizona mountains I found myself alert in a fresh way—to the winds, the skies, the climate, the food, the trails. My senses became engaged and active. Internally, I recognized the changes in my sense of peace and joy, a resonance to my surroundings that is so easily missed when we allow ourselves to be swallowed by apathy that can arise as we age.

In Chaco Canyon, I became hypervigilant while climbing that mesa wall, aware of my legs, my fingers, my breath, my muscles. I felt the pain and the exhilaration caused by my fear. My breath was choppy and ragged. I was fully present while hanging onto that wall. My interior self processed and calculated my survival with super speed. I paid attention with intention!

While in the Cotswolds, I became alert to the rain pelting me, to the pungent smells from the animals grazing in the fields, to the colors of the flowers that grew with abandon along the edges of our paths, to the low hum of voices in the pubs. The interior journey found delight in a childlike freedom to be ignorant and wistful at the same time. You know, like when we climbed on a bicycle for the first time and rode it both with fear and abandon!

The Vermont pilgrimage surely demanded my full attention as I watched over Tom and focused on those tricky trails so he would not stumble. Our marriage played through my head during those daily walks, the hiking and the rutted trails serving as metaphors for our thirty some odd years together.

All four of these pilgrimages created in me a form of Mindful Awareness even before I was exposed to this meditation tool. My exterior experiences and my interior musings merged into a collage of insights that have become fodder for reflection and growth. Aging for so many seniors tends to steal our energy, our attention and our courage away from us, leaving behind in its wake depression, regrets, loneliness, boredom, even despair. Mindfulness that leads us to be present to each moment of our life and to others shapes the healing balm for the negativity of aging.

Again, this is only half the story. While I have become aware that my attention is much more heightened from the work I did on the pilgrimages, my task is to apply this awareness to the world I inhabit. My true calling is to become a wise Presence in what is remaining of my life because each of us lives more fully when we live as Presence to each other and to our world.

Recently I received an online newsletter from a long-time friend whose wife had died. His agony of loss is so tangible in his grief-soaked words, "My own mind and soul have become numb and a strange incapacitation has gripped me. Sinking as I did, the deep joy I simply took for granted in our marriage and life together blurred into two numb souls bound together but drifting into darkness. A numb soul inclines unwittingly toward sadness and loneliness, often called despair." This poignant confession wrenches my heart for my friend as he finds himself abiding in the depths of anguish for the loss of his beloved. How is it possible to climb out of such a deep and dark hole? This grief our friend is experiencing requires so much of him.

Making ourselves present to life and others can help us recover from these negative places in our minds and hearts so that our lives might become full and rich again—not without some hard work, mind you. But it is possible to find hope again on the other side of depression, illness, or death, a renewed sense of adventure and purpose. My belief is, however, that staying alert to the woes of aging does require of us maximum courage to thwart our darkest thoughts and emotions. It is easy to fall into denial of the aging reality. Facing and negotiating our way through the pain and suffering we experience is just as important as living intentionally toward the pleasures and adventures.

All of my pilgrimages formed a menagerie of experiences, each teaching me awareness at a new level. One can be present while washing dishes, attending a political meeting, writing a book, hosting a potluck barbecue, or watching a rainbow in the sky. In the final analysis, as I see it, the definition of Presence goes like this:

Presence (as we age) is the urgency to resist the insistent pull to make ourselves invisible while deliberately choosing to be available to the fullness of life, all of it.

Think about this for a moment. When do you find yourself absent from the moment in which you are living? How many times a day do you absent yourself from what is going on around you, from persons you live with, from nature, from your tasks or community? What is it about our predilection to easily and often enter a drifting zone that creates in us the tendency to hide from being aware and present to the moment?

I can only encourage you to try something with me. Take your next lived moment and accept what just happened as just part of being alive, regardless of whether you just took out the trash, mowed the lawn, played with a grandchild, met with a new chiropractor, planned a neighborhood block gathering, drove to the car wash, even cut your finger while chopping an onion. Do not judge the action; accept and allow the current moment simply to be what it is. While paying attention to what occurred, mentally list as many of the details about that experience as you are able. What were you consciously aware of while involved in this activity? Upon reflection what did you miss?

Once you have completed this list, reconnoiter inside your interior self, exploring your thoughts and emotions. What do they offer you by way of insight? How much of the time spent involved in the action were you actually present? How much of the time were you absent? Did you tune into what your emotions were telling you, your intuitions and even your imagination, or did you just ignore your interior signals altogether? Mindfulness starts with a lack of judgment about everything going on around us, moving toward acceptance of the realities of life, this journey in which we find ourselves living within our being.

A reminder: Wisdom is not tied to age or experience. The oldest adult on the planet could be one of the most foolish persons alive. The growth of wisdom in a particular human being is not an automatic response to the number of years or lived experiences.

As I wrote this chapter, my spouse asked me if a child could be wise. My response was a resounding, "Yes!"

If a child has faced her mortality in some fashion, the result is often a child with "wisdom beyond her years." A child with a terminal illness or one who has suffered a severe trauma, physical or emotional, so often speaks wisdom to us, don't they? The acknowledgment that we are mortal can awaken us so our wisdom might ignite, even in a child.

I will share one final example of "making Presence" that is changing my perspective on becoming wise. So many people in my world serve and assist me (such as clerks, waiters, mechanics, attendants, assistants, secretaries, nurses—the list is endless), making my life richer and better. In my awareness space I have begun intentionally to ask and remember a name, learn something about the person, and seek a way to connect with them on the human level before our encounter is over. This small exercise has had huge results. I have noticed that suddenly I am not dismissed as an "old person," and they have not been dismissed by me as someone simply making my life easier.

The most recent experience took place with a doctor's nurse who had a curt, no-nonsense temperament. The first time she met me, she did not smile and could not be cajoled into a discussion. On the second visit I finally discovered something through small talk that sparked an interest in her. I began to banter with her about a symbol she was wearing and saw the first light of recognition on her face. It took three visits to that doctor's office before I moved from being a number with a condition, to a person with a story. In my world of needing nurses she has become a person with a real story. After a year of encounters with this young woman, I now genuinely care for her as a human being who matters to me in my world. Now, when I leave a call on her phone about a need I have, we have a relationship. Her return calls are warm and she "knows" me as I "know" her. Presence. We have become humans on a mission together.

And the same can occur for those brief encounters we have. Another nurse, this time a male, a decade younger, with streaks of gray running through his hair, lively brown eyes and a warm smile decorating his face. When I needed a medical test, Gerard escorted me to the examination room. On the way down the long, winding, nondescript, beige halls we chatted, quickly learning that we share a common medical condition. During the procedure, which included some pain for me, he held my hand as I cried. Before the hour had passed, we were calling each other by name, sharing our stories of life, love, and venture. We are likely not to see each other again, but our time together had been compassionate, engaged, and human. Presence. This magical tool for aging wisely actually works.

Bob's Wisdom of Presence spoke to me, even years after he was gone.

Aging into the Wisdom Years calls forth our gratitude for life itself. We are here! We are present! We are alive! Even in our most horrific agony, we exist. Being absent from our lived moments is to squander the gift of life we have received. If we are empty or fearful, we have nothing to offer ourselves, others, or the world. Living intentionally means living ripe, ready, fully formed, whole! Aging is akin to ripeness, a coming to fruition of all we have seen, known, thought, experienced, heard, lived, danced, ventured. I stated earlier that the Wisdom Years are a calling. Seeking wisdom is not a hobby. Any venture that nurtures our calling to be wise is a valuable, meaningful, critical-to-life experience.

Our soul journey insists that we refuse to allow the fruit of our lives to rot on the vine. Rather, we are to bring our Authentic Presence to fullness and wholeness. This includes our senior years when we have so much to offer. The only way through this tricky labyrinth is to become vulnerable and open, willing to take risks, to adapt and to accept change. This is not an easy task at a time in life when we desperately desire security, comfort and familiarity. But the reward for our willingness to seek the grand adventure emerges with vivid audacity and courage because we dared to live with purpose and Presence. Only our intentional aging creates the mystery, magic, and meaning in our lives.

The adventure of aging is caught in the tension between grief and delight. No senior lives without grief. It is a constant companion because loss laces its gnarled fingers around our hearts and minds during these later years. As we age the way in which we face loss defines the quality of our living. Yet there is a quixotic response to loss: delight. We come close in these years to the child we once were. If we are present to the unfolding of our days, we can rediscover the charm and delight in those small, simple moments and pleasures.

The Wisdom Years call courageous seniors to step into the land of intentional aging with a sense that the rest of life is an adventure, a pilgrimage, a journey. Life is at one level a grand mystery, just as Fitzmaurice stated. At another level it's the most ordinary event possible, taking place only in the moment because in reality this is all there is available to us, this current moment. Living between these two realities sets the space where the Life of Wisdom is formed and transformed.

I have come to see this adventure into aging not only as a privilege, but also as a responsibility. Boomers are retiring by the thousands each day. Thus we must ask ourselves whether and how we intend to contribute to the health and wisdom of the human drama. Never before in the story of humankind has there been such a massive group of Elderlies inhabiting the planet. We have an obligation to offer Planet Earth our best wisdom and a new model for aging and dying, with grace and gratitude, courage and compassion. We seniors need to get this right, do our aging well, to create a lively, vital, healthy home for the Millennials who are coming behind us with their own hopes and dreams to participate in a peaceful and fruitful life. This task is our duty to the future.

I close this book with a poem I wrote a few months after I completed my pilgrimage year. For one brief moment I was mindful enough to witness a spectacular sunset that spoke to me of my living and my passing.

One Red Streak

Blazing across the intrepid skies
One Red Streak
gleams so bravely against the fading blue—
this Day is almost done,
while clinging tentatively to the
waning moments of Light
that dance across the purple mountain peaks
and settle with excitement and precision upon
the gnarled juniper treetops.
My eyes squint, with one final attempt
to wrestle the last drop of beauty from this day.
My soul moans as it recognizes that the residue
of this fleeting light-show
slyly announces the tragic brevity of our lives.
At this time of day
caution is undesirable—
the scarlet hues of the sunset
beckon us into the secrets of the dark night ahead,
where we dare to be bold
as we approach our own sure death.
May we pass in a blaze, like this One Red Streak
that dashes across the curved canvas of sky,
flung from the earth into the universe
where only the dust of the Cosmic Mind
rests and remembers—
How beautiful it is to be alive!

EPILOGUE

No sooner had I completed my manuscript than chapter 1 of this book shoved its way into my life. Without too much concern, I took a calcium heart scan just to satisfy my primary care doctor who was not happy with my earlier cholesterol numbers. Since my numbers have bounced between okay and worrisome for years, I was not in a panic. After the scan the technician, with a furrowed brow, sat down beside me to go over my results. I remember nothing else that he said except two words, "widow maker."

After the doctor saw the numbers on the scan, she instructed me to take a stress test. I wasn't worried about this either. I walk briskly five miles a day, most days of the week, at altitude on trails throughout my neighborhood in Santa Fe, New Mexico. My Fitbit is my best friend as it fills the blackened screen with tiny explosions on my wrist each day when I pass the ten thousand steps milestone. I knew I would pass the stress test with little effort. And I did—with flying colors! However…

Fortunately, I had previously scheduled a follow-up appointment with a cardiologist—just in case. Grudgingly, I kept the date and went to see him, only to expect him to send me home without much information except to perhaps scold me about eating too much cheese. However, after an intense set of questions and a brief discussion, he abruptly left the room. His nurse returned within moments and asked, "Is tomorrow at 8:00 a.m., okay?"

"For what?" I was alarmed at this point.

"For an angiogram," she said crisply.

From this point on the next twenty-four hours are mostly a blur. Caught in the web of anesthesia, I woke up at one point long enough to hear my spouse tell me that I now have a stent in my heart after the doctor found 90 percent blockage in my "widow maker" artery. Added to this procedure had also been an angioplasty in one of my smaller arteries. To block the shock of the news, I promptly fell back into a drug-induced sleep.

Within two weeks, I also learned I am living with an aneurysm in my heart. Isn't it a shame we don't have an extra heart like our kidneys, so one can go bad but we still have one that works? In one day I went from being a woman on a thrilling life journey, with her health and retirement intact (so I believed) to someone with a cabinet full of pills, a restricted regimen for eating, a demanding exercise schedule and the odd notion that I can die at any moment.

So that's the story. Now how do I take my own work in this book seriously and live with a sense of adventure, intention, meaning, and joy while preparing for a reckoning with my own mortality? All I can say to you, the reader, is this: had I not walked the four pilgrimages and given myself those precious life-altering experiences, I do not believe I would be doing very well with all of these dramatic changes in my life. I suspect I would be depressed, afraid, and full of uncertainly. But somehow the pilgrimages and the life lessons I learned from them have rescued me from the negative side of my new story.

So what has changed in my interior life? I am more pragmatic now about my own death. It seems closer and more real. At the same time, I practice mindfulness more frequently, with greater commitment and pleasure. I stare at the mountains a bit more, listen to the birds, watch the playful New Mexico clouds, enjoy my work with just a touch more Presence. I am so deeply grateful that I had the courage to challenge myself and walk the pilgrimages. The lessons I learned are now saving me from my worst thoughts, emotions and nightmares. Instead, I am living intentionally. The aging project has been successful, at least for me. This is all I can tell you. Try it. What have you got to lose?

BIBLIOGRAPHY

Abbey, Edward. *Desert Solitaire.* New York: Random House, 1968.

Becker, Ernest. *The Denial of Death.* New York: The Free Press, 1973.

Botton, de Alain. *The Course of Love.* New York: Simon & Schuster, 2016.

Brother Lawrence. *The Practice of the Presence of God.* Translated by Donald Attwater. Springfield, IL: Templegate, 1974.

Bruna, John. *The Wisdom of a Meaningful Life.* Las Vegas: Central Recovery Press, 2016.

Burdick, Alan. *Why Time Flies.* New York: Simon & Schuster, 2017.

Coelho, Paulo. *The Pilgrimage.* New York: Harper Perennial, 1998.

Fitzmaurice, Simon. *It's Not Yet Dark.* Boston: Houghton Mifflin Harcourt, 2014.

Friedman, Thomas. *Thank You for Being Late.* New York: Farrar, Strause and Giroux, 2016.

Gawande, Atul. *Being Mortal.* New York: Metropolitan Books, 2014.

Harari, Yuval Noah. *Sapiens.* New York: HarperCollins, 2015.

Harris, Sam. *Waking Up.* New York: Simon & Schuster, 2014.

Horne, William W. *Portraits of Courage.* Washington, DC: AARP Magazine, Vol. 60, No. 3C, April/May 2017.

Iliff, Brenda. *Alcohol Abuse Soars for Older Americans.* Washington, DC: AARP Bulletin, October 2017.

Joyce, Rachel. *The Love Song of Miss Queenie Hennessy.* New York: Random House, 2014.

Joyce, Rachel. *The Unlikely Pilgrimage of Harold Fry.* New York: Random House, 2013.

Lathem, Edward, C. Editor. *The Poetry of Robert Frost.* New York, Holt, Rinehart and Winston, 1969.

Lief, Judy. *Death, the Greatest Teacher.* The Lion's Roar Magazine, November 2017.

Love, Robert, ed. Washington, DC: AARP Magazine, Vol. 61, No. 1C, January, 2018

O'Donohue, John. *Anam Cara: A Book of Celtic Wisdom.* New York: HarperCollins, 2004.

Rohr, Richard. *Falling Upward.* San Francisco, California: Jossey-Bass, 2011.

Taylor, Barbara Brown. *Leaving Church.* New York: Harper One, 2007.

Whyte, David. *River Flow.* Langley, WA: Many Rivers Press, 2007.

About the Author

Barbara S. Boyd is retired from her institutional career. Previously she served at the University of Oklahoma as the director of Outreach and as faculty for the religious studies program. Dr. Boyd is also a retired Presbyterian (PCUSA) clergywoman, having served in various functions within four churches during her years in ministry.

In retirement, Barbara spends her time involved in writing projects, including poetry. She also spends time involved in a science and religion study group that constantly expands her horizons. For recreation, she prefers yoga, hiking, walking, or biking. Leisure activities include reading, films, gardening, hosting meals for neighbors and friends. And finally, the proverbial attachment to grandchildren fills the heart and soul of this author.

Barbara is married to Tom, and they reside in Santa Fe, New Mexico. Between them, they have four children and eight astonishing grandchildren, scattered from Texas to Scotland and Germany.